IN TIME OF WAR

Compiled by Pat Edwards and Wendy Body

In Flanders Fields

In Flanders fields the poppies blow
Between the crosses, row on row,
That mark our place; and in the sky
The larks, still bravely singing, fly
Scarce heard amid the guns below.

We are the Dead. Short days ago
We lived, felt dawn, saw sunset glow,
Loved and were loved, and now we lie
In Flanders fields.

John McCrae

Acknowledgements

We are grateful to the following for permission to reproduce copyright material; Jonathan Cape Ltd for Chapters 6 & 7 from *The Silver Sword* by Ian Serraillier; the author's agents for the poem 'Innocent's Song' from *Collected Poems* by Charles Causley (pub Macmillan); C J Fulcher on behalf of the author for the poem 'Peace' by Richard Eburne from *First Year Poetry Anthology 1986-87*, compiled by C J Fulcher, produced by Chepstow Comprehensive School: Victor Gollancz Ltd for an extract from *Carrie's War* by Nina Bawden & an extract from *Z for Zachariah* by Robert C O'Brien, (c) Robert C O'Brien 1975; the author's agents for an extract from *The Summer of My German Soldier* by Bette Greene (pub Hamish Hamilton Ltd); Hamish Hamilton Ltd for an extract from *Eagle's Egg* by Rosemary Sutcliffe; Hodder & Stoughton (Australia) Pty Ltd for the story 'The Angel With A Mouth-Organ' from *The Angel With A Mouth-Organ* by Christobel Mattingley (pub 1984); the author's agents for the poem 'The Second World War' from *Collected Poems* by Elizabeth Jennings (pub Macmillan); Penguin Books Ltd & the author's agents for an extract from *Goodnight Mister Tom* by Michelle Magorian (pub Kestrel Books, 1981), copyright (c) Michelle Magorian, 1981; Punch Publications Ltd for the poem 'In Flanders Field' by John McCrae, first published in *Punch*, 8th Dec. 1915; Vallentine, Mitchell & Co Ltd for an extract from *The Diary of Anne Frank* by A Frank.

We are grateful to the following for permission to reproduce photographs and newspaper extracts: Australian War Memorial (photo Damien Parer), page 19; *The Daily Mirror* (front page) 5.8.1914, Syndication International/John Frost, page 80; *Daily Sketch* (front page) 4.9.1939, International Thomson Corporation/John Frost, page 81 *below right*; *Evening Chronicle* (front page) 3.9.1939, Thomson Regional Newspapers/John Frost, page 81 *above* and *below left*; Hulton-Deutsch Collection, page 5; Popperfoto, pages 2/3 *background*, 40; *The Western Morning News* (front page) 5.8.1914, John Frost, page 80 *above left, above right* and *below*; Nancy Wake (Port Macquarie, NSW, Australia), page 4.

Cover: *The Daily Mail* (page 6) 31.12.1940, Solo Syndication/John Frost.

Illustrators, other than those acknowledged with each story, include Pat Sirninger pp. 1, 112; Louise Metcalfe pp. 6-7; Mayer Winter pp. 52-3; Linda Cerkvenik pp. 82-3; David Wong pp. 106-9.

Contents

ALIAS the White Mouse

In 1944 Nancy Wake commanded 7000 resistance fighters. Trained in unarmed combat, she was parachuted in behind enemy lines and led guerilla raids on factories and Gestapo headquarters.

Who was 'the White Mouse'? During the Second World War, a twenty-nine year old Australian woman called Nancy Wake was known to both her enemies and her allies by her code name 'the White Mouse'. But such a code name for such a courageous and even deadly young woman was completely misleading. Nancy was far from being mouse-like!

What did 'the White Mouse' do? Before her twenty-first birthday in 1933, Nancy left Australia and sailed to Europe. All she had was £300 and not much confidence. She found herself working in Paris as a freelance journalist for American newspapers. Paris at that time was becoming very unsettled and fearful of the rumblings of German discontent from just across the border.

Nancy, however, was very happy. She had met and married a Frenchman, Henry Fiocca. Perhaps it was because of Henry that Nancy grew to love France and her people. Her husband taught her to speak French and the rough language of the Marseille waterside workers — did he have a premonition of what was to happen?

When the German army invaded France, Nancy decided to help the Allies and took great personal risks. She began by helping British soldiers to escape from Marseille. Her house became known as a 'safe house' — that is, a place where secret messages could be passed on as part of an underground network of information. It was also a safe place for people on the run to hide.

Nancy began to act as a courier, too, travelling up and down France, carrying secret messages. And, together with many others, she became an invaluable link in a chain of people that over $2\frac{1}{2}$ years saw 1037 men escape to freedom. But that wasn't all! Time was running out. The Germans were on the White Mouse's tail. Nancy was now being hunted. She fled to Spain, and after a short bout in prison there, escaped to England where she was approached by British Intelligence. They trained her to be an undercover agent and one dark night in March 1944, she dropped by parachute back into France. Her mission? To help arm, train and co-ordinate 7000 guerilla fighters. (That's when the 'rough language' came in handy!) Nancy successfully worked with her men, attacking and killing German army officials, but not without a price. Her husband was captured, tortured and killed by German army officials anxious to flush the White Mouse from her hole. They never succeeded.

Adolf Hitler addressing German soldiers and youth.

Peace

War is full of people dying,
War is full of relatives crying,
Peace makes people happy, not sad,
Things like Peace are good, not bad.

War is dismal, dark and bloody,
In trenches deep, but small and muddy.
Peace is beautiful, quiet and clean,
When people are kind, no one is mean.

War is terrible, no matter what kind,
Peace is a lot nicer, I'm sure you'll find.
Peace and happiness come hand in hand,
Sparkling and golden like the desert sand.

Peace and joy are like a team,
Each one like a bright sunbeam.

Richard Eburne
aged 12

In the Lions' Den

This is part of the story of a Polish family and what happened to them during World War II. Early in 1940, Joseph Balicki, headmaster of a Warsaw primary school, had been snatched from his family and sent off to a prison camp in South Poland. His Swiss wife, Margrit, and three children — Ruth, nearly thirteen, Edek, eleven and Bronia, three — stay on at the schoolhouse. One fateful night, the Nazi storm-troopers return . . .

That night there was an inch of snow on the roofs of Warsaw. Ruth and Bronia were asleep in the bedroom next to their mother's. Edek's room was on the top floor, below the attic. He was asleep when the Nazi soldiers broke into the house, but he woke up when he heard a noise outside his door. He jumped out of bed and turned the handle. The door was locked. He shouted and banged on it with his fists, but it was no use. Then he lay down with his ear to the floor and listened. In his mother's room the men were rapping out orders, but he could not catch a word that was said.

In the ceiling was a small trapdoor that led into the attic. A ladder lay between his bed and the wall. Quietly he removed it, hooked it under the trap, and climbed up.

Hidden between the water tank and the felt jacket round it was his rifle. He was a member of the Boys' Rifle Brigade and had used it in the siege of Warsaw. It was loaded. He took it out and quickly climbed down to his room.

The noise in the room below had stopped. Looking out of the window into the street, he saw a Nazi van waiting outside the front door. Two storm troopers were taking his mother down the steps, and she was struggling.

8

Quietly Edek lifted the window sash till it was half open. He dared not shoot in case he hit his mother. He had to wait till she was in the van and the doors were being closed.

His first shot hit a soldier in the arm. Yelling, he jumped in beside the driver. With the next two shorts Edek aimed at the tyres. One punctured the rear wheel, but the van got away, skidding and roaring up the street. His other shots went wide.

With the butt of his rifle he broke down the door and ran down to his sisters. They were locked in, too. He burst open the door.

Bronia was sitting up in bed and Ruth was trying to calm her. She was almost as distraught herself. Only the effort to comfort Bronia kept her from losing control.

"I hit one of the swine," said Edek.

"That was very silly of you," said Ruth. "They'll come back for us now."

"I couldn't let them take Mother away like that," said Edek. "Oh, be quiet, Bronia! Howling won't help."

"We must get away from here before they come back," said Ruth.

With some difficulty she dressed Bronia, while Edek went into the hall to fetch overcoats and boots and fur caps.

There was no time for Ruth to dress properly. She put on a coat over her nightdress and wound a woollen scarf round Bronia.

"We can't get out the front way," said Edek. "There's another van coming. I heard the whistle."

'What about the back?" said Ruth.

"The wall's too high. We'd never get Bronia over. Besides, there are Nazis billeted in that street. There's only one way — over the roof.'

"We'll never manage that," said Ruth.

"It's the only way," said Edek. "I'll carry Bronia. Be quick — I can hear them coming."

He picked up the sobbing Bronia and led the way upstairs. He was wearing his father's thick overcoat over his pyjamas, a pair of stout boots on his bare feet, and his rifle slung on his back.

When they were all up in the attic, he smashed the sky-light.

"Now listen, Bronia," said Edek. "If you make a sound, we shall never see Mother again. We shall all be killed."

"Of course we shall see her again," Ruth added. "But only if you do as Edek says."

He climbed through the skylight on to the slippery roof. Ruth handed Bronia up to him, then followed herself. The bitterly cold air made her gasp.

I can't carry you yet, Bronia," said Edek. "You must walk behind me and hold on to the rifle. It doesn't matter if you slip, if you hold on to the rifle. And don't look down."

The first few steps — as far as the V between the chimney and the roof ridge — were ghastly. Edek made a dash for it, grabbed the telephone bracket and hauled himself up, with Bronia clinging on behind. She was speechless with terror. He reached back and hauled Ruth up after him.

After a few moments' rest, they slid down a few feet on to a flat part that jutted out, a sort of parapet.

The roof ridge lay between them and the street, so they could not see what was happening down there. But they could hear shouting, the whine of cars, the screech of brakes.

Luckily for them, all the houses on this side of the school were joined together in one long terrace, otherwise they could not have got away. Even so, it was a miracle that none of their slips and tumbles ended in disaster.

They must have gone fully a hundred yards when the first explosion shook the air. A sheet of the fire leapt up from their home into the frosty night sky. They fell flat in the snow and lay there. The roof shook, the whole city seemed to tremble. Another explosion. Smoke and flames poured from the windows. Sparks showered into the darkness.

"Come along," said Edek. "We shan't let them have us now."

With growing confidence they hurried along the roof-tops. At last, by descending a twisted fire escape, they reached street level. On and on they hurried, not knowing or caring where they went so long as they left those roaring flames behind them.

They did not stop till the fire was far away and the pale winter dawn was breaking.

They took shelter in the cellar of a bombed house. Exhausted, huddled together for warmth, they slept till long after midday, when cold and hunger woke them.

They made their new home in a cellar at the other end of the city. They had tunnelled their way into it. From the street it looked like a rabbit's burrow in a mound of rubble, with part of a wall rising behind. On the far side there was a hole in the lower part of the wall, and this let in light and air as well as rain.

When they asked the Polish Council of Protection about their mother,
they were told she had been taken off to Germany to work on the land.
Nobody could say which part of Germany. Though they went many times
to ask, they never found out any more. "The war will end soon," they
were told. "Be patient, and your mother will come back."

But the war dragged on, and their patience was to be sorely tried.

They quickly made their new home as comfortable as they could. Edek,
who could climb like a monkey, scaled three storeys of a bombed building
to fetch a mattress and some curtains. The mattress he gave to Ruth and
Bronia. The curtains made good sheets. On wet days they could be used
over the hole in the wall to keep the rain out. With floorboards he made
two beds, chairs and a table. With bricks from the rubble he built a wall
to divide the cellar into two rooms, one to live in and one to sleep in. He
stole blankets from a Nazi supply dump, one for each of them.

Here they lived for the rest of that winter and the following spring.

Food was not easy to find. Ruth and Bronia had green Polish ration cards and were allowed to draw the small rations that the Nazis allowed. But, except when Edek found casual work, they had no money to buy food. Edek had no ration card. He had not dared to apply for one, as that would have meant disclosing his age. Everyone over twelve had to register, and he would almost certainly have been carried off to Germany as a slave worker. Whenever possible they ate at the soup kitchens which Polish Welfare had set up. Sometimes they begged at a nearby convent. Sometimes they stole from the Nazis or scrounged from their garbage bins. They saw nothing wrong in stealing from their enemies, but they were careful never to steal from their own people.

War had made Edek sharp and self-reliant for his years. Ruth was slower to adapt herself to the new life. At first, during that long-drawn-out winter and the biting winds of early spring, it seemed as if she were too young to take on responsibility. But she learned gradually. She saw that Edek was always cheerful — because he was always busy. She knew she must get out of the habit of leaving all the practical details to him. One thing she could do was to make Bronia less miserable. She remembered that Bronia had always loved drawing. Ever since her little fist had been able to hold a pencil, she had delighted her father with her scribbles. So Ruth encouraged her to go on drawing now. They had no pencils or paper, but they had the cellar walls and plenty of charred wood from which to make charcoal. Bronia drew what she saw. Soon the walls were covered with pictures of people queueing outside the soup kitchen and of children playing hide and seek among the ruins.

Then Ruth started a school. She invited other lost children, of Bronia's age and a little older. While Edek was out at work or finding food, she told them stories in the cellar. When she ran out of stories, the others took their turn. She made them speak out clearly, without mumbling. One day at the soup kitchen she talked about her school. Next time she went she was given slates and chalk and a pocket Bible. News of these presents spread like a heath fire, and soon she had a mob of urchins outside the cellar window begging to be allowed to join the school. But there was only room for twelve, and very reluctantly she had to turn them away.

Ruth was a born teacher. She could hold the children spellbound for as long as she liked. She varied the work as much as possible, giving the mornings to lessons and the afternoons to play.

The day started with a Bible story. She read it herself, with the children round her — three to a blanket if it was cold. Next came reading and writing, followed by a break in the open air. Up they shot from their rabbits' warren into the sunlight. They ran down the street to the wooden fence which they called 'the Riviera'. Here they would sit in a long line, pressing their backs to the sun-drenched wood, soaking up the warmth till their bodies were glowing all over. On sunless days they played a brisk game before returning to the cellar for another story.

They liked the stories from the Old Testament best. Their favourite was always Daniel in the lions' den. They enjoyed it just as a story, but for Ruth it had a deeper meaning. She thought of it as the story of their own troubles. The lions were the cold and the hunger and the hardships of their life. If only they were patient and trustful like Daniel, they would be delivered from them. She remembered a picture of Daniel that her mother had once given her. He was standing in the dungeon, with his hands chained behind him and his face lifted towards a small barred window high above his head. He was smiling and did not notice the lions that prowled about his feet, powerless to touch him. At night she liked to fall asleep with this picture in her mind. She could not always see it clearly. Sometimes Daniel's face was clouded and the light from the window fell upon the lions. They were scowling and snarling, and they filled her dreams with terror.

15

In the early summer they left the city and went to live in the woods outside. It was cold at night out in the open. They slept huddled together in their blankets under an oak tree which Edek had chosen for the shelter of its branches. There was not much rain that summer, though they had one or two drenchings in May. After that Edek cut down some branches, lashed them together and made a lean-to. This was thick enough to keep out all but the heaviest rain.

Life was much healthier here than in the city. The sun browned their limbs. There were plenty of other families to play with, some of them Jews who had escaped from the Warsaw ghetto. They could run about freely and hold their classes under the trees, without having to keep a look-out for police patrols. Sometimes Ruth had as many as twenty-five in her school. She would have taken more, but they had no paper, very few slates, and no books at all. Occasionally they received a smuggled copy of a secret journal specially published for children by the Polish Underground press. It was called *Biedronka*, "The Ladybird", and was full of the kind of stories and pictures and jokes that children enjoy. The grubby finger marks showed that other families had seen it before them. When Ruth's children had finished with it, there was nothing left but a few tattered strips.

Because of the kindness of the peasants, food was more plentiful. Though they were forbidden to store food or to sell it to anyone but the Nazis, they gave the children whatever they could spare. They hid it, too, in cellars, in hay-stacks, in holes in the ground. With the help of the older children they smuggled it to the towns and sold it to the Poles on the black market.

Edek was one of the chief smugglers. In return for his services, he was given all the food he needed for the family. One of his dodges was to go off to town with pats of butter sewn into the lining of his coat. But he could only do this on cool days or at night. On hot days the butter melted. So he preferred to work at night if he could. In time the Germans became wary and posted patrols on all the main roads into the city. After that he cut across country, using paths and rough tracks. He was well aware of the penalties if he was caught. A younger child might get away with a beating. But boys as strong as he was would be carried off to Germany, for the Nazis were getting short of labour at home.

Another of Edek's dodges was the cartload of logs which he drove into the suburbs.

Some of the logs were split, their centres scraped out and packed with butter and eggs, then glued together again.

Once he drove his cartload into a police patrol, which was searching everything on the road. They emptied the logs on to the pavement. Edek didn't stay to see if the glue would stand up to that treatment. He dived into the crowd and made off. Police whistles were blowing and the chase had started, when some kind friend lifted him up and pitched him head first into a garbage cart. Here he lay hidden, under cinders and dust and rotting vegetables.

After that, Edek did all his smuggling at night.

There came a morning, towards the end of August, when he failed to return. Ruth questioned other families in the forest, but no one had seen him. After some days of searching, she traced him to a village ten miles away. Edek had called at a house there while the secret police were searching for hidden stores. They had found cheese sewn into the lining of his coat. After setting fire to the house, they had taken him away in the van, with the house owner as well.

Ruth returned to the forest with a heavy heart, dreading to break the news to Bronia.

Edek had been their life-line. Food, clothes, money — they depended on him for all these. In the city he had made a home out of a ruin. In the woods no tree gave better shelter than the oak he had chosen. And after dark, when the wind blew cold and the damp oozed out of the ground, none knew better than he how to keep the fire in untended till dawn, so that the glow from the embers should warm them all night as they slept.

Now Ruth and Bronia must fend for themselves. It was an ordeal before which the bravest spirit might quail.

by Ian Serraillier
illustrated by Andrew Cunningham

Photograph by Damien Parer of an Australian soldier
leading a blind and wounded soldier across a river in
Papua New Guinea during World War II.

Two Nights of FEAR

*W*hen the Nazi invaders of the Netherlands intensified their persecution of the Jews, the Frank family — mother, father and daughters 16 year old Margot and 13 year old Anne — went into hiding in the sealed off rooms at the back of an Amsterdam building from which Mr Frank had run his business. They share the hideaway with four other people — Mr and Mrs Van Daan, their fifteen year old son, Peter (who brings his cat Mouschi), and Albert Dussel, a dentist whose wife was out of the country when war broke out. Mr Frank's staff, Mr Kraler, Mr Koophuis, Miep Van Stanten and the teenage typist, Elli Vossen, have agreed to help the fugitives with food and supplies. Apart from Miep's husband, Henk, these people are the only ones to know of the existence of the hidden rooms.

Anne had begun her diary in June 1942, deciding to write in it as if talking to an imaginary friend named Kitty and has continued to pour out her thoughts and fears during the long, weary months of their confinement. Everything depends on their ability to keep quiet at all times and to conceal all evidence of their presence. The unrelenting strain has made life difficult for all, but the situation is eased for Anne and Peter who, in the past two years, have fallen in love.

Tuesday, 11th April, 1944

Dear Kitty,

My head throbs, I honestly don't know where to begin.

On Friday (Good Friday) we played Monopoly, Saturday afternoon too. These days passed quickly and uneventfully. On Sunday afternoon, on my invitation, Peter came to my room at half-past four; at a quarter-past five we went to the front attic, where we remained until six o'clock. There was a beautiful Mozart concert on the radio from six o'clock until a quarter-past seven. I enjoyed it all very much, but especially the *Kleine Nachtmusik*. I can hardly listen in the room because I'm always so inwardly stirred when I hear lovely music.

On Saturday evening Peter and I went to the front attic together and, in order to sit comfortably, we took with us a few divan cushions that we were able to lay our hands on. We seated ourselves on one packing-case. Both the case and the cushions were very narrow, so we sat absolutely squashed together, leaning against other cases. Mouschi kept us company too, so we weren't unchaperoned.

Suddenly, at a quarter to nine, Mr. Van Daan whistled and asked if we had one of Dussel's cushions. We both jumped up and went downstairs with cushion, cat and Van Daan.

A lot of trouble arose out of this cushion, because Dussel was annoyed that we had one of his cushions, one that he used as a pillow. He was afraid that there might be fleas in it and made a great commotion about his beloved cushion! Peter and I put two hard brushes in his bed as a revenge. We had a good laugh over this little interlude!

Our fun didn't last long. At half-past nine Peter knocked softly on the door and asked Daddy if he would just help him upstairs over a difficult English sentence. "That's a blind," I said to Margot, "anyone could see through that one!" I was right. They were in the act of breaking into the warehouse. Daddy, Van Daan, Dussel and Peter were downstairs in a flash. Margot, Mummy, Mrs. Van Daan and I stayed upstairs and waited.

Four frightened women just have to talk, so talk we did, until we heard a bang downstairs. After that all was quiet, the clock struck a quarter to ten. The colour had vanished from our faces, we were still quiet, although we were afraid. Where could the men be? What was that bang? Would they be fighting the burglars? Ten o'clock, footsteps on the stairs: Daddy, white and nervy, entered, followed by Mr. Van Daan. "Lights out, creep upstairs, we expect the police in the house!"

There was no time to be frightened: the lights went out, I quickly grabbed a jacket and we were upstairs. "What has happened? Tell us quickly!" There was no one to tell us, the men having disappeared downstairs again. Only at ten past ten did they reappear; two kept watch at Peter's open window, the door to the landing was closed, the swinging bookcase shut. We hung a jersey round the night light, and after that they told us:

Peter had heard two loud bangs on the landing, ran downstairs and saw there was a large plank out of the left half of the door. He dashed upstairs, warned the "Home Guard" of the family and the four of them proceeded downstairs. When they entered the warehouse, the burglars were in the act of enlarging the hole. Without further thought Van Daan shouted: "Police!"

A few hurried steps outside, and the burglars had fled. In order to avoid the hole being noticed by the police, a plank was put against it, but a good hard kick from outside sent it flying to the ground. The men were perplexed at such impudence, and both Van Daan and Peter felt murder welling up within them; Van Daan beat on the ground with a chopper, and all was quiet again. Once more they wanted to put the plank in front of the hole. Interruption! A married couple outside shone a torch through the opening, lighting up the whole warehouse. "Hell!" muttered one of the men, and now they switched over from their rôle of police to that of burglars. The four of them sneaked upstairs, Peter quickly opened the doors and windows of the kitchen and private office, flung the telephone on to the floor and finally the four of them landed behind the swinging bookcase. — End of Part One.

The married couple with the torch would probably have warned the police: it was Sunday evening, Easter Sunday, no one at the office on Easter Monday, so none of us could budge until Tuesday morning. Think of it, waiting in such fear for two nights and a day! No one had anything to suggest, so we simply sat there in pitch darkness, because Mrs. Van Daan in her fright had unintentionally turned the lamp right out; talked in whispers, and at every creak one heard "Sh! sh!"

It turned half-past ten, eleven, but not a sound; Daddy and Van Daan joined us in turns. Then a quarter-past eleven, a bustle and noise downstairs. Everyone's breath was audible, otherwise no one moved. Footsteps in the house, in the private office, kitchen, then . . . on our staircase. No one breathed audibly now, footsteps on our staircase, then a rattling of the swinging bookcase. This moment is indescribable. "Now we are lost!" I said, and could see us all being taken away by the Gestapo that very night. Twice they rattled at the bookcase, then there was nothing, the footsteps withdrew, we were saved so far. A shiver seemed to pass from one to another, I heard someone's teeth chattering, no one said a word.

There was not another sound in the house, but a light was burning on our landing, right in front of the bookcase. Could that be because it was a secret bookcase? Perhaps the police had forgotten the light? Would someone come back to put it out? Tongues loosened, there was no one in the house any longer — but perhaps there was someone on guard outside.

Next we did three things: we went over again what we supposed had happened, we trembled with fear, and we had to go to the lavatory. The buckets were in the attic, so all we had was Peter's tin wastepaper basket. Van Daan went first, then Daddy, but Mummy was too shy to face it. Daddy brought the wastepaper basket into the room, where Margot, Mrs. Van Daan and I gladly made use of it. Finally Mummy decided to do so too. People kept on asking for paper — fortunately I had some in my pocket!

The tin smelt ghastly, everything went on in a whisper, we were tired, it was twelve o'clock. "Lie down on the floor then and sleep." Margot and I were each given a pillow and one blanket; Margot lying just near the store-cupboard and I between the table legs. The smell wasn't quite so bad when one was on the floor, but still Mrs. Van Daan quietly fetched some chlorine, a tea towel over the pot serving as a second expedient.

Talk, whispers, fear, stink, people breaking wind, and always someone on the pot: then try to go to sleep! However, by half-past two I was so tired that I knew no more until half-past three. I awoke when Mrs. Van Daan laid her head on my foot.

"For Heaven's sake, give me something to put on!" I asked. I was given something, but don't ask what — a pair of woollen knickers over my pyjamas, a red jumper, and a black skirt, white over-socks and a pair of sports stockings full of holes. Then Mrs. Van Daan sat in the chair and her husband came and lay on my feet. I lay thinking till half-past three, shivering the whole time, which prevented

Van Daan from sleeping. I prepared myself for the return of the police then we'd have to say that we were in hiding; they would either be good Dutch people, then we'd be saved, or the N.S.B.,* then we'd have to bribe them!

"In that case, destroy the radio," sighed Mrs. Van Daan. "Yes, in the stove!" replied her husband. "If they find us, then let them find the radio as well!"

"Then they will find Anne's diary," added Daddy. "Burn it then," suggested the most terrified member of the party. This, and when the police rattled the cupboard door, were my worst moments. "Not my diary, if my diary goes, I go with it!" But luckily Daddy didn't answer.

There is no object in recounting all the conversations that I can still remember; so much was said. I comforted Mrs. Van Daan, who was very scared. We talked about escaping and being questioned by the Gestapo, about ringing up, and being brave.

"We must behave like soldiers, Mrs. Van Daan. If all is up now, then let's go for Queen and Country, for freedom, truth and right, as they always say on Radio Orange. The only thing that is really rotten is that we get a lot of other people into trouble too."

Mr. Van Daan changed places again with his wife after an hour, and Daddy came and sat beside me. The men smoked non-stop, now and then there was a deep sigh, then someone went on the pot and everything began all over again.

Four o'clock, five o'clock, half-past five. Then I went and sat with Peter by his window and listened, so close together that we could feel each other's bodies quivering; we spoke a word or two now and then, and listened attentively. In the room next door they took down the black-out. They wanted to ring up Koophuis at seven o'clock and get him to send someone round. Then they wrote down everything they wanted to tell Koophuis over the 'phone. The risk that the police on guard at the door, or in the warehouse, might hear the telephone was very great, but the danger of the police returning was even greater.

The points were these:

Burglars broken in: police have been in the house, as far as the swinging bookcase, but no further.

Burglars apparently disturbed, forced open the door in the warehouse and escaped through the garden.

Main entrance bolted, Kraler must have used the second door when he left. The typewriters and adding machine are safe in the black case in the private office.

Try to warn Henk and fetch the key from Elli, then go and look around the office — on the pretext of feeding the cat.

Everything went according to plan. Koophuis was rung up, the typewriters which

*The Dutch National Socialist Movement.

we had upstairs were put in the case. Then we sat round the table again and waited for Henk or the police.

Peter had fallen asleep and Van Daan and I were lying on the floor, when we heard loud footsteps downstairs. I got up quietly: "That's Henk."

"No, no, it's the police," some of the others said.

Someone knocked at the door, Miep whistled. This was too much for Mrs. Van Daan, she turned as white as a sheet and sank limply into a chair; had the tension lasted one minute longer she would have fainted.

Our room was a perfect picture when Miep and Henk entered, the table alone would have been worth photographing! A copy of *Cinema and Theatre*, covered with jam and a remedy for diarrhoea, opened at a page of dancing girls, two jam pots, two partly eaten pieces of bread, a mirror, comb, matches, ash, cigarettes, tobacco, ash-tray, books, a pair of pants, a torch, toilet-paper, etc. etc., lay jumbled together in variegated splendour.

Of course Henk and Miep were greeted with shouts and tears. Henk mended the hole in the door with some planks, and soon went off again to inform the police of the burglary. Miep had also found a letter under the warehouse door from the night watchman Slagter, who had noticed the hole and warned the police, whom he would also visit.

So we had half an hour to tidy ourselves. I've never seen such a change take place in half an hour. Margot and I took the bedclothes downstairs, went to the W.C., washed and did our teeth and hair. After that I tidied the room a bit and went upstairs again. The table there was already cleared, so we ran off some water and made coffee and tea, boiled the milk and laid the table for lunch. Daddy and Peter emptied the potties and cleaned them with warm water and chlorine.

At eleven o'clock we sat round the table with Henk, who was back by that time, and slowly things began to be more normal and cosy again. Henk's story was as follows:

Mr. Slagter was asleep, but his wife told Henk that her husband had found the hole in our door when he was doing his tour round the canals, and that he had fetched a policeman, who had gone through the building with him. He would be coming to see Kraler on Tuesday and would tell him more then. At the police station they knew nothing of the burglary yet, but the policeman had made a note of it at once and would come and look round on Tuesday. On the way back Henk happened to meet our greengrocer at the corner, and told him that the house had been broken into. "I know that," he said quite coolly. "I was passing last evening with my wife and saw the hole in the door. My wife wanted to walk on, but I just had a look in with my torch; then the thieves cleared at once. To be on the safe side, I didn't ring up the police, as with you I didn't think it was the thing to do. I don't know anything, but I guess a lot."

Henk thanked him and went on. The man obviously guesses that we're here, because he always brings the potatoes during the lunch hour. Decent chap!

It was one by the time Henk had gone and we'd finished the washing-up. We all went for a sleep. I awoke at a quarter to three and saw that Mr. Dussel had already disappeared. Quite by chance, and with my sleepy eyes. I ran into Peter in the bathroom; he had just come down. We arranged to meet downstairs.

I tidied myself and went down. "Do you still dare to go to the front attic?" he asked. I nodded, fetched my pillow and we went up to the attic. It was glorious weather, and soon the sirens were wailing; we stayed where we were. Peter put his arm round my shoulder, and I put mine round his and so we remained, our arms round each other, quietly waiting until Margot came to fetch us for coffee at four o'clock.

We finished our bread, drank lemonade and joked (we were able to again), and everything else went normally. In the evening I thanked Peter because he was the bravest of us all.

None of us has ever been in such danger as that night. God truly protected us; just think of it — the police at our secret cupboard, the light on right in front of it, and still we remained undiscovered.

If the invasion comes, and bombs with it, then it is each man for himself, but in this case the fear was also for our good, innocent protectors. "We are saved, go on saving us!" That is all we can say.

This affair has brought quite a number of changes with it. Mr. Dussel no longer sits downstairs in Kraler's office in the evenings, but in the bathroom instead. Peter goes round the house for a check-up at half-past eight and half-past nine. Peter isn't allowed to have his window open at nights any more. No one is allowed to pull the plug after half-past nine. This evening there's a carpenter coming to make the warehouse doors even stronger.

Now there are debates going on all the time in the "Secret Annexe". Kraler reproached us for our carelessness. Henk, too, said that in a case like that we must never go downstairs. We have been pointedly reminded that we are in hiding, that we are Jews in chains, chained to one spot, without any rights but with a thousand duties. We Jews mustn't show our feelings, must be brave and strong, must accept all inconveniences and not grumble, must do what is within our power and trust in God. Some time this terrible war will be over. Surely the time will come when we are people again, and not just Jews.

Who has inflicted this upon us? Who has made us Jews different to all other people? Who has allowed us to suffer so terribly up till now? It is God that has made us as we are, but it will be God, too, who will raise us up again. If we bear all this suffering and if there are still Jews left, when it is over, then Jews, instead of being doomed, will be held up as an example. Who knows, it might even be our religion from which the world and all peoples learn good, and for that reason and that reason only do we have to suffer now. We can never become just Netherlanders, or just English, or representatives of any country for that matter, we will always remain Jews, but we want to, too.

Be brave! Let us remain aware of our task and not grumble, a solution will come, God has never deserted our people. Right through the ages there have been Jews, through all the ages they have had to suffer, but it has made them strong too; the weak fall, but the strong will remain and never go under!

During that night I really felt that I had to die, I waited for the police, I was prepared, as the soldier is on the battlefield. I was eager to lay down my life for the country, but now, now I've been saved again, now my first wish after the war is that I may become Dutch! I love the Dutch, I love this country, I love the language and want to work here. And even if I have to write to the Queen myself, I will not give up until I have reached my goal.

I am becoming still more independent of my parents, young as I am, I face life with more courage than Mummy; my feeling for justice is immovable, and truer than hers. I know what I want, I have a goal, an opinion, I have a religion and love. Let me be myself and then I am satisfied. I know that I'm a woman, a woman with inward strength and plenty of courage.

If God lets me live, I shall attain more than Mummy ever has done, I shall not remain insignificant, I shall work in the world and for mankind!

And now I know that first and foremost I shall require courage and cheerfulness!

Yours, ANNE

by Anne Frank
illustrated by Margarette Chellew

'Two nights of fear' is from **The Diary of Anne Frank.** *Anne's diary ends on 1 August 1944. The group were discovered and arrested on 4 August 1944. The Jewish prisoners were sent to the horrific Auschwitz and, in February 1945, the two Frank girls caught typhus and died. Peter was never heard of again.*

EVACUEES

HE threw up all over Miss Fazackerly's skirt. He had been feeling sick ever since they left the main junction and climbed into the joggling, jolting little train for the last lap of their journey, but the sudden whistle had finished him.

Such a noise — it seemed to split the sky open. "Enough to frighten the dead," Miss Fazackerly said, mopping her skirt and Nick's face with her handkerchief. He lay back limp as a rag and let her do it, the way he always let people do things for him, not lifting a finger. "Poor lamb," Miss Fazackerly said, but Carrie looked stern.

"It's all his own fault. He's been stuffing his face ever since we left London. Greedy pig. *Dustbin.*"

He had not only eaten his own packed lunch — sandwiches and cold sausages and bananas — but most of Carrie's as well. She had let him have it to comfort him because he minded leaving home and their mother more than she did. Or had looked as if he minded more. She thought now that it was just one of his acts, put on to get sympathy. Sympathy and chocolate! He had had all her chocolate, too! "I knew he'd be sick," she said smugly.

"Might have warned me then, mightn't you?" Miss Fazackerly said. Not unkindly, she was one of the kindest teachers in the school, but Carrie wanted to cry suddenly. If she had been Nick she would have cried, or at least put on a hurt face. Being Carrie she stared crossly out of the carriage window at the big mountain on the far side of the valley. It was brown and purple on the top and green lower down; streaked with silver trickles of water and dotted with sheep.

Sheep and mountains. "Oh it'll be such fun," their mother had said when she kissed them good-bye at the station. "Living in the country instead of the stuffy old city. You'll love it, you see if you don't!" As if Hitler had arranged this old war for their benefit, just so that Carrie and Nick could be sent away in a train with gas masks slung over their shoulders and their names on cards round their necks. Labelled like parcels — Caroline Wendy Willow and Nicholas Peter Willow — only with no address to be sent to. None of them, not even the teachers, knew where they were going. "That's part of the adventure," Carrie's mother had said, and not just to cheer them up: it was her nature to look on the bright side. If she found herself in Hell, Carrie thought now, she'd just say, "Well, at least we'll be *warm*."

Thinking of her mother, always making the best of things (or pretending to: when the train began to move she had stopped smiling) Carrie nearly did cry. There was a lump like a pill stuck in her throat. She swallowed hard and pulled faces.

The train was slowing. "Here we are," Miss Fazackerly said. "Collect your things, don't leave anything. Take care of Nick, Carrie."

Carrie scowled. She loved Nick, loved him so much sometimes that it gave her a pain, but she hated to be told to do something she was going to do anyway. And she was bored with Nick at the moment. That dying-duck look as he struggled to get his case down from the rack! "Leave it to me, silly baby," she said, jumping up on the seat. Dust flew and he screwed up his face. "You're making me sneeze," he complained. "Don't *bounce*, Carrie."

They all seemed to have more luggage than when they had started. Suitcases that had once been quite light now felt as if they were weighed down with stones. And got heavier as they left the small station and straggled down a steep, cinder path. Carrie had Nick's case as well as her own and a carrier bag with a broken string handle. She tucked it under one arm, but it kept slipping backwards and her gas mask banged her knee as she walked.

"Someone help Caroline, please," Miss Fazackerly cried, rushing up and down the line of children like a sheep dog. Someone did — Carrie felt the carrier bag go from under her arm, then one suitcase.

It was a bigger boy. Carrie blushed, but he wasn't a Senior: he wore a cap like all the boys under sixteen, and although he was tall, he didn't look very much older than she was. She glanced sideways and said, "Thank you *so* much," in a grown-up voice like her mother's.

He grinned shyly back. He had steel-rimmed spectacles, a few spots on his chin. He said, "Well, I suppose this is what they call our ultimate destination. Not much of a place, is it?"

They were off the cinder track now, walking down a hilly street where small, dark houses opened straight on to the pavement. There was sun on the mountain above them, but the town was in shadow; the air struck chill on their cheeks and smelled dusty.

"Bound to be dirty," Carrie said. "A coal-mining town."

"I didn't mean dirt. Just that it's not big enough to have a good public library."

It seemed a funny thing to bother about at the moment. Carrie said, "The first place was bigger. Where we stopped at the junction." She peered at his label and read his name. Albert Sandwich. She said, "If you came earlier on in the alphabet you could have stayed there. You only just missed it, they divided us after the R's. Do your friends call you Ally, or Bert?"

"I don't care for my name to be abbreviated," he said. "Nor do I like being called Jam, or Jelly, or even Peanut Butter."

He spoke firmly but Carrie thought he looked anxious.

"I hadn't thought of sandwiches," she said. "Only of the town Sandwich in Kent, because my granny lives there. Though my dad says she'll have to move now in case the Germans land on the coast." She thought of the Germans landing and her grandmother running away with her things on a cart like a refugee in a newspaper picture. She gave a loud, silly laugh and said, "If they did, my gran 'ud give them What For. She's not frightened of anyone, I bet she could even stop Hitler. Go up on her roof and pour boiling oil down!"

Albert looked at her, frowning. "I doubt if that would be very
helpful. Old people aren't much use in a war. Like kids — best
out of the way."

His grave tone made Carrie feel foolish. She wanted to say it
was only a joke, about boiling oil, but they had arrived at a
building with several steps leading up and told to get into single
file so that their names could be checked at the door. Nick was
waiting there, holding Miss Fazackerly's hand. She said, "There
you are, darling. There she is, didn't I tell you?" And to Carrie,
"Don't lose him again!"

She ticked them off on her list, saying aloud, "Two Willows,
One Sandwich."

33

Nick clung to Carrie's sleeve as they went through the door into a long, dark room with pointed windows. It was crowded and noisy. Someone said to Carrie, "Would you like a cup of tea, bach? And a bit of cake, now?" She was a cheerful, plump woman with a sing-song Welsh voice. Carrie shook her head; she felt cake would choke her. "Stand by there, then," the woman said. "There by the wall with the others, and someone will choose you."

Carrie looked round, bewildered, and saw Albert Sandwich. She whispered, "What's happening?" and he said, "A kind of cattle auction, it seems."

He sounded calmly disgusted. He gave Carrie her suitcase, then marched to the end of the hall, sat down on his own, and took a book out of his pocket.

Carrie wished she could do that. Sit down and read as if nothing else mattered. But she had already begun to feel ill with shame at the fear that no one would choose her, the way she always felt when they picked teams at school. Suppose she was left to the last! She dragged Nick into the line of waiting children and stood, eyes on the ground, hardly daring to breathe. When someone called out, "A nice little girl for Mrs Davies, now," she felt she would suffocate. She looked up but unfocused her eyes so that passing faces blurred and swam in front of her.

Nick's hand tightened in hers. She looked at his white face and the traces of sick round his mouth and wanted to shake him. No one would take home a boy who looked like that, so pale and delicate. They would think he was bound to get ill and be a trouble to them. She said in a low, fierce voice, "Why don't you smile and look nice," and he blinked with surprise, looking so small and so sweet that she softened. She said, "Oh it's all right, I'm not cross. I won't leave you."

Minutes passed, feeling like hours. Children left the line and were taken away. Only unwanted ones left, Carrie thought. She and Nick, and a few tough-looking boys, and an ugly girl with a squint who had two little sisters. And Albert Sandwich who was still sitting quietly on his suitcase, reading his book and taking no notice. *He* didn't care! Carrie tossed her head and hummed under her breath to show she didn't either.

Someone had stopped in front of her. Someone said, "Surely you can take two, Miss Evans?"

"Two girls, perhaps. Not a boy and a girl, I'm afraid. I've only the one room, see, and my brother's particular."

Particular about what, Carrie wondered. But Miss Evans looked nice; a little like a red squirrel Carrie had once seen, peering round a tree in a park. Reddish brown hair and bright, button eyes, and a shy, quivering look.

Carrie said, "Nick sleeps in my room at home because he has bad dreams sometimes. I always look after him and he's no trouble at all."

Miss Evans looked doubtful. "Well, I don't know what my brother will say. Perhaps I can chance it." She smiled at Carrie. "There's pretty eyes you have, girl! Like green glass!"

Carrie smiled back. People didn't often notice her when Nick was around. *His* eyes were dark blue, like their mother's. She said, "Oh, Nick's the pretty one, really."

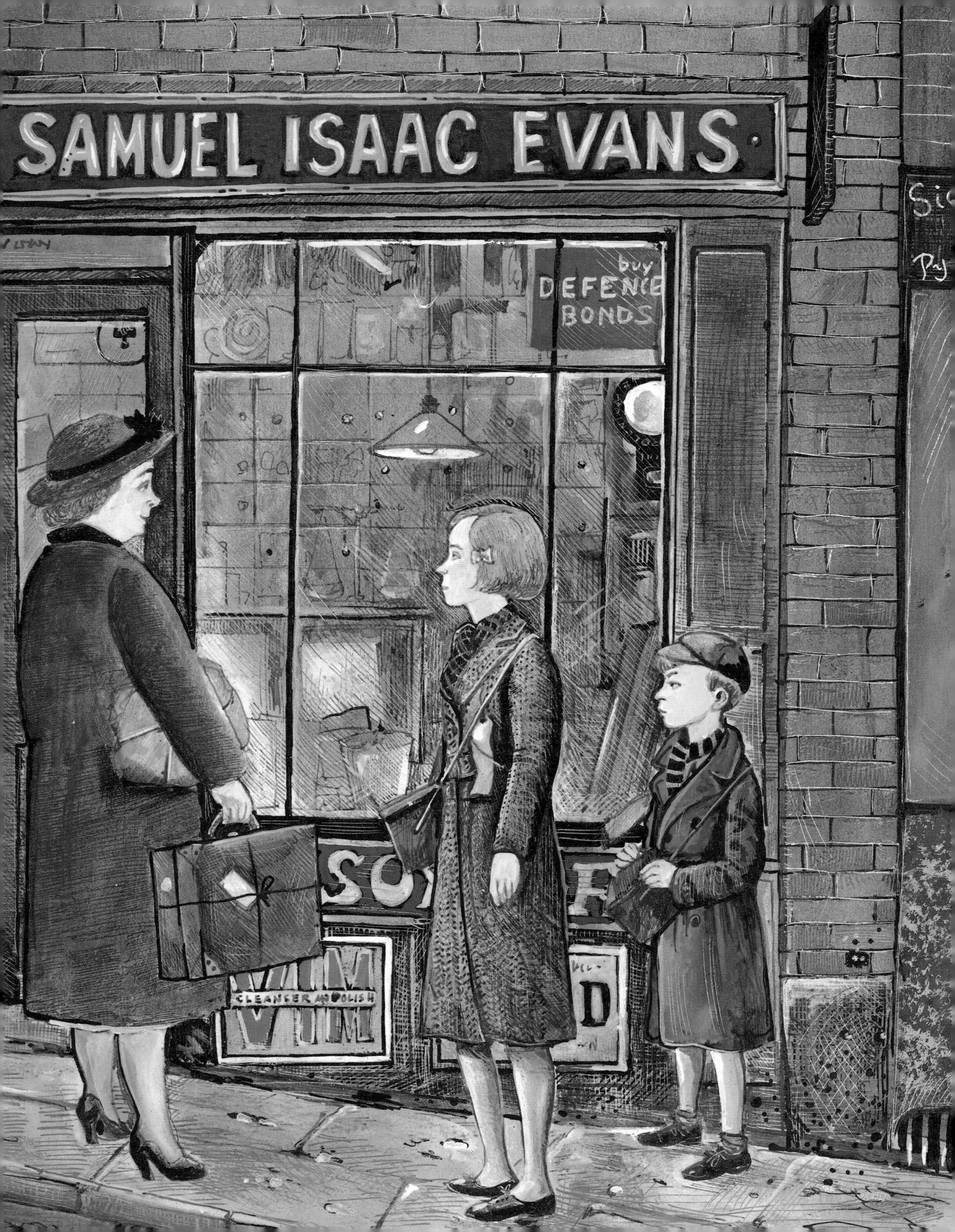
SAMUEL ISAAC EVANS
buy
DEFENCE
BONDS

Miss Evans walked fast. She was a little woman, not much taller than Carrie, but she seemed strong as a railway porter, carrying their cases as if they weighed nothing. Out of the hall down the street. They stopped outside a grocery shop with the name SAMUEL ISAAC EVANS above the door and Miss Evans took a key from her bag. She said, "There's a back way and you'll use that, of course, but we'll go through the front for the once, as my brother's not here."

The shop was dim and smelled mustily pleasant. Candles and tarred kindling, and spices, Carrie thought, wrinkling her nose. A door at the back led into a small room with a huge desk almost filling it. "My brother's office," Miss Evans said in a hushed voice and hurried them through into a narrow, dark hall with closed doors and a stair rising up. It was darker here than the shop and there was a strong smell of polish.

Polished linoleum, a shining, glass sea, with rugs scattered like islands. Not a speck of dust anywhere. Miss Evans looked down at their feet. "Better change into your slippers before we go up to your bedroom."

"We haven't got any," Carrie said. She meant to explain that there hadn't been room in their cases but before she could speak Miss Evans turned bright red and said quickly, "Oh, I'm so sorry, how silly of me, why should you? Never mind, as long as you're careful and tread on the drugget."

A strip of white cloth covered the middle of the stair carpet. They trod on this as they climbed; looking back from the top, Carrie saw the marks of their rubber-soled shoes and felt guilty, though it wasn't her fault. Nick whispered, "She thinks we're poor children, too poor to have slippers," and giggled.

Carrie supposed he was right. Nick was good at guessing what people were thinking. But she didn't feel like giggling; everywhere was so tidy and clean it made her despair. She thought she would never dare touch anything in this house in case she left marks. She wouldn't dare *breathe* — even her breath might be dirty!

Miss Evans was looking at Nick. "What did you say, dear?" she asked, but didn't wait for an answer. "Here's the bathroom," she said — proudly, it seemed. "Hot and cold running water, *and* a flush toilet. And your room, just by here."

It was a small room with two narrow beds and a hooked rug between them. A wardrobe and a wicker chair and a large, framed notice on the wall. The black letters said, *The Eye Of The Lord Is Upon You*.

Miss Evans saw Carrie looking at this. She said, "My brother is very strong Chapel. So you'll have to be especially good, Sundays. No games or books, see? Except the Bible, of course."

The children stared at her. She smiled shyly. "It may not be what you're used to but it's better to get things straight from the start, isn't it? Mr Evans is a good man, but strict. Manners and tidiness and keeping things clean. He says dirt and sloppy habits are an insult to the Lord. So you will be good, won't you? You look like good children."

It was almost as if she were pleading with them. Asking them to be good so that *she* wouldn't get into trouble. Carrie was sorry for her, though she felt very uncomfortable. Neither she nor Nick were particularly tidy; at home, in their warm, muddly house, no one had expected them to be. Milly, their maid, always picked up their toys and made their beds and put their clothes away. Carrie said, "We'll try to be good, Miss Evans."

"Call me Auntie," Miss Evans said. "Auntie Louise. Or Auntie Lou, if that's easier. But you'd best call my brother Mr Evans. You see, he's a Councillor." She paused and then went on in the same proud tone she had used when she showed them the bathroon, "Mr Evans is a very important man. He's at a Council meeting just now. I think I'd best give you your supper before he comes back, hadn't I?"

Written by Nina Bawden
Illustrated by Chris Price

The Second

World War

The voice said "We are at War"
And I was afraid, for I did not know what this meant.
My sister and I ran to our friends next door
As if they could help. History was lessons learnt
With ancient dates, but here
Was something utterly new,
The radio, called the wireless then, had said
That the country would have to be brave. There was much to do.
And I remember that night as I lay in bed
I thought of soldiers who
Had stood on our nursery floor
Holding guns, on guard and stiff. But war meant blood
Shed over battle-fields, Cavalry galloping. War
On that September Sunday made us feel frightened
Of what our world waited for.

Elizabeth Jennings

THE EAGLE'S EGG

Quintus is a young Standard-bearer with the Ninth Legion stationed at Eburacum (York) in second-century Roman Britain. At this time the eagle standard was used by all Roman legions throughout the empire. The Standard-bearer marched at the head of the foot soldiers, carrying this symbol of Rome's power and glory, and Quintus was proud of his rank. But now he needs to gain promotion to centurion, for only centurions are allowed to marry, and Quintus has fallen in love with Cordaella, a British girl. It seems he must earn it the hard way, by serving in one of General Agricola's campaigns to subdue the Painted People in the wilds of Calidonia (Scotland). But there has been no word of a campaign and even the discovery that Vedrix, Cordaella's brother, will not stand in their way, does not solve the problem. Until one day . . .

I was standing before the piled writing-table in the Headquarters Office, where Dexius Valens the Senior Centurion had sent for me, waiting for him to notice that I was there. After a while he looked up from the scatter of tablets and papyrus rolls before him, and said, "Ah, Standard-bearer. — Yes, the General Agricola is at Corstopitum over-seeing the arrangements for this summer's Caledonian Campaign. The order has just come through. We march to join him in three days."

So that was that. All town leave was stopped, of course, and I never even got to see Cordaella to say farewell to her. Couldn't write her a note, either, because of course she couldn't read anyway. The best I could do was to scratch a few lines to Vedrix and ask him to read them to her — I thought I could trust him — and get one of the mule-drivers to take the letter down into the town the next day.

And three days later, leaving the usual holding-garrison behind us, we marched out for Corstopitum.

A Legion on the march — that's something worth the seeing; the long winding column, cohort after cohort, the cavalry wings spread on either side and the baggage train following after. A great serpent of mailed men, red-hackled with the crests of the officers' helmets, and whistling whatever tune best pleases them at the moment — "Payday" perhaps, or "The Emperor's Wineskins", or "The Girl I kissed at Clusium", to keep the marching time. Four miles to the hour, never slower, never faster, uphill and down, twenty miles a day . . . . And me, marching up at the head, right behind the Legate on his white horse, carrying the great Eagle of the Legion, with the sunlight splintering on its spread wings; and its talons clutched on the lighting-jags of Jupiter, and the gilded laurel wreaths of its victories . . . .

Aye, I was the proud one, that day! For I'd seen Cordaella among the crowd that gathered to see us off, and she had seen me and waved to me. And I was through with garrison duty and going to join the fighting, and win my promotion and maybe make a name for myself and come back with the honours shining on my breast; and all for my girl Cordaella. And my breast swelled as though the honours were already there. What a bairn I was, what a boy with my head chock-full of dreams of glory, for all the great lion-skin that I wore over my armour, and the size of my hands on the Eagle shaft, and my long legs eating up the Northward miles!

But it was three years and more before we came marching back; and there were times when I came near to forgetting Cordaella for a while, though never quite.

We joined Agricola with the Twentieth Legion at Corstopitum, and marched on North across the great Lowland hills until we were

joined by the main part of the Second and the Fourteenth that had come up through the western country of last summer's campaigning.

Then we headed on for the broad Firth that all but cuts Caledonia in half. The Fleet met us there, and we spent the rest of the summer making a naval base. You need something of that sort for supplies, and support, when you can't be sure of your land lines of communication behind you. We saw a bit of fighting from time to time, but seemingly the Lowland chiefs were still too busy fighting with each other, to make a strong show against us, so mostly it was just building; first the supply base, and then with the winter scarce past, a string of turf and timber forts right across the low-lying narrows of the land.

Sick and tired we got of it, too, and there began to be a good deal of grumbling. I mind Lucius, a mate of mine growling into his supper bannock that he might as well have stayed at home and been a builder's labourer — and me trying to give him the wink that the Cohort Commander was standing right behind him. It's odd, the small daft things not worth remembering, that one remembers across half a lifetime . . .

But in the next spring, when we started the big push on into the Highlands, we found a difference.

Somehow, sometime in that second winter, the Caledonians had found the leader they needed to hammer them into one people. Calgacus, his name was, I never saw him, not until the last battle; but I got so that the bare mention of his name would have me looking over my shoulder and reaching for my sword. It was the same with all of us, especially when the mists came down from the high tops or rain blotted out the bleak country as far as a man could see. Oh yes, we saw plenty enough fighting that summer, to make up for any breathing space we'd had in the two before.

Agricola was too cunning a fox to go thrusting his muzzle up into the mountains, with every turf of bog-cotton seemingly a war-painted warrior in disguise, waiting to close the glens like a trap on his tail. Instead, he closed them himself, with great forts in the mouths of each one where it came down to the eastern plain. That way, there was no risk of the tribes swarming down unchecked to take us in the rear or cut our supply lines afer we had passed by.

We got sullen-sick of fort building, all over again, yes; especially with our shoulder-blades always on the twitch for an arrow between them. The Ninth wintered at Inchtuthil, the biggest of the forts. The place was not finished, but we sat in the middle and went on building it round us, which is never a very comfortable state of things, in enemy country. We lost a lot of men in one way and another; and the old ugly talk of the Ninth being an unlucky Legion woke up and began to drift round again.

It might have been better if the Legate had not had a convenient bout of stomach trouble and gone south to winter in Corstopitum. I didn't envy Senior Centurion Dexius left in command. It was our third winter in the wilds, and we were sick of snow and hill mists, and the painted devils sniping at us from behind every gorse-bush; and we wanted to be able to drink with our friends in a wine shop, and walk twenty paces without wondering what was coming up behind us. And we cursed the Legate for being comfortable in Corstopitum, and grew to hate the sight of each other's faces.

I began to smell trouble coming, sure as acorns grow on oak trees.

And then one day when we had almost won through to spring, some of the men broke into the wine store and were found drunk on watch. They were put under guard, ready to be brought up before the Senior Centurion next day. And everyone knew what that meant. He'd have been within his rights to order the death penalty; but being Daddy Dexius, who could be relied on to be soft in such matters, they would probably get off with a flogging. Even so, it would be the kind of flogging that spreads a man flat on his face in the sick block for three days afterwards.

All the rest of that day you could feel the trouble like nearing thunder prickling in the back of your neck. And in the middle of supper, it came.

Being the Eagle bearer, I ate in the Centurions' mess-hall, though in the lowest place there, next to the door; and I hadn't long sat down when the noise began.

It wasn't particularly loud, but there was an ugly note to it; a snarling note; and in the midst of it someone shouting, "Come on, lads, let's get the prisoners out!'' and other voices taking up the cry.

I remember Dexius's face as he got up and strode past me to the door; and suddenly knowing that we had all been quite wrong about him; that he wasn't soft at all. More the kind of man who gets a reputation for being good-tempered and fair-game, because he knows that if he once lets his temper go and hits somebody he probably won't leave off till he's killed them.

I had only just started my supper, so I snatched a hard-boiled duck's egg from a bowl on the table and shoved it down the front of my uniform, and dashed out with the rest.

Outside on the parade-ground a crowd was gathering. Some of them had makeshift torches. The flare of them was teased by the thin wind that was blowing, and their light fell ragged on faces that were sullen and dangerous. Vipsanius the duty centurion was trying to deal with the situation, but he didn't seem to be having much success, and the crowd was getting bigger every moment.

Daddy Dexius said coolly, "What goes on here, Centurion?"

"They're refusing to go on watch, Sir," said Vipsanius. I mind he was sweating up a bit, despite the edge to the wind.

"We've had enough of going on watch in this dog-hole, night after filthy night!" someone shouted.

And his mates backed him up. "How much longer are we going to squat here, making a free target of ourselves for the blue painted barbarians?"

"If Agricola wants to fight them, why doesn't he come up and get things going?"

"Otherwise why don't we get out of here and go back where we came from?"

Men began shouting from all over the crowd, bringing up all the old soldiers' grievances about pay and leave and living conditions. "We've had enough!" they shouted, "We've had enough!"

"You'll have had more than enough, and the Painted People down on us, if you don't break up and get back on duty!" Vipsanius yelled back at them.

But the sullen crowd showed no sign of breaking up or getting back on duty. And suddenly, only half-believing, I understood just how ugly things might be going to turn. Not much harm done up to now, but if something, anything, tipped matters even a little in the wrong direction, the whole crowd could flare up into revolt, and revolt has a way of spreading that puts a heath-fire to shame.

Centurion Dexius said, "Thank you, Centurion, I will take over now." And then he glanced round for me. "Standard-bearer."

"Here, Sir," says I, advancing smartly.

"Go and fetch out the Eagle, and we'll see if that will bring them to their senses."

I left him standing there, not trying to shout them down or anything, just standing there, and went to fetch the Eagle.

In the Saccellum, part office and part treasury and part shrine, the lamp was burning on the table where the duty centurion would sit all night with his drawn sword before him — when not doing Rounds or out trying to quell a riot — and the Eagle on its tall shaft stood against the wall, with the Cohort standards ranged on either side of it.

I took it down; and as I did so its upward shadow, cast by the lamp on the table engulfed half the chamber behind it, as though some vast dark bird had spread wing and come swooping forward out of the gloom among the rafters. Used though I was to the Eagle standard, that great swoop of dark wings made me jump half out of my skin. But it was not the moment to be having fancies. I hitched up the Eagle into Parade Position, and out I went with it.

The Senior Centurion had quieted them down a bit; well, the look on his face would have quieted all Rome on a feast day; and when they saw the Eagle, their growling and muttering died away till I could hear a fox barking, way up the glen, and the vixen's scream in answer. But they still stood their ground, and I knew the quiet wouldn't last. And there was I, standing up with the Eagle, not knowing quite what to do next; and truth to tell, beginning to feel a bit of a fool. And then suddenly it came to me; what I had to do next; and I pulled out the duck's egg from inside my tunic and held it up.

And, "Now look what you've done, you lot!" said I, "Behaving like this you've upset the Eagle so much it's laid an egg!"

I have noticed more than once in the years since then, that it is sometimes easier to swing the mood of a whole crowd than it is to swing the mood of one man on his own. Aye, a dicey thing is a crowd.

There was a moment of stunned silence, and then someone laughed, and someone else took up the laugh, and then more and more, a roar of laughter and a surge of stamping and back-slapping that swept away all that had gone before.

by Rosemary Sutcliff
illustrated by Peter Schmidli

51

f the wanderings of Odysseus were the perfect soap opera, then the Trojan War and the siege of Troy have all the makings of an award winning mini-series.

Imagine this drama unfolding on your TV screen!

It opens with trouble at the wedding of Peleus and Thetis. It's his second marriage, but it's a pretty grand affair because she's a sea goddess. It seems they'd committed the social sin of not inviting Eris, goddess of discord. Her nose properly out of joint, Eris turns up anyway and throws an apple inscribed, "To the Fairest" amongst the guests. Immediately it's claimed by not one, but three, reigning beauties. There's Hera (who has seniority because she's the wife of Zeus), Athena (goddess of wisdom) and Aphrodite, who is goddess of love.

Before the ladies start scratching each other's eyes out, they ask a handsome young fellow named Paris to decide who should have the apple. Each of the beauties tries to bribe him. Hera offers the throne of Asia, Athena promises honour in war and Aphrodite says she'll give him the most beautiful woman in the world for his wife. Completely ignoring the fact that he's already married to Oenone, the likely lad gives the apple to Aphrodite.

But there's a catch. The beauty queen title is held by Helen—and she's already married to Menelaus, King of Sparta. However, Paris, whose morals are not what they ought to be, persuades Helen that she's foreordained to be his wife and the guilty pair elope. Paris decides to take her home to Dad, who just happens to be Priam, King of Troy. And so the scene is set.

Instead of being grateful to be rid of a faithless wife, Menelaus decides he wants Helen back. He calls up his pals (all the other kings of Greece) and a great war force is assembled with his brother Agamemnon as commander-in-chief. Amongst those on the Greek side are Odysseus (remember him?) and Achilles — son of Peleus and Thetis (so that gives you an idea of how long it's taken for all these shenanigans to have taken place). The Trojan heavies are Paris (who has caused all the rumpus), Hector (Paris' older brother) and Aeneas, son of Aphrodite.

The Greeks lay siege to Troy, which is well fortified, and nothing much happens for nearly ten years, except for a lot of squabbling amongst the allies. (Would you believe one of them commits suicide in a rage when he's not given the dead Achilles' armour?) It was Paris' arrow that killed Achilles, so it's only fitting that Paris should meet his just desserts soon after. He's wounded and he's tactless enough to ask Oenone to nurse him. Understandably, she gives him the cold shoulder and he dies. Full of remorse she kills herself and the place is littered with bodies. (Where's Helen? You may well ask. Fickle jade, she's off marrying Paris' younger brother, Hector having been polished off some time ago).

By now everyone's sick of funerals and the Greeks want to go home. It's time for deceit and strategy (in other words, a little bit of dirty work). Odysseus comes up with a plan. They build a huge wooden horse and then, making plenty of noise, pack up all their belongings and take off—leaving the horse outside the city gates. Human nature being what it is, the Trojans can't contain their curiosity. The minute the coast is clear they rush out to examine the fascinating wooden statue. And who should be lurking in the undergrowth, but a sad and sorry Greek named Sinon who claims he's been left behind because he got on the wrong side of Odysseus. Ever so casually, he mentions the Greeks had built the wooden horse as an offering to Athena, but then they'd been warned that the minute the horse entered Troy, death and destruction will strike the Greek army.

This is just what the Trojans want to hear so, completely ignoring the advice of one of their priests, they drag the huge statue inside the gates. Before there's time for second thoughts, a big party celebrating the end of the siege breaks out. In the middle of the night, when all the Trojans are dead asleep or lying in a drunken stupor, Sinon opens a secret door in the horse. Surprise! Surprise! It's filled with armed men. What's more, the Greek army has sneaked back under cover of darkness and the minute the soldiers inside have killed the sentries and opened the gates, they sweep in. There's a big finale of bloodshed and burning—and the siege of Troy is over!

Oh yes, want to know what happened to Helen? After all that, Menelaus still took her back and she lived to a ripe old age. Doesn't seem fair, does it?

A BIT OF A LONER

The year is 1939. World War II has broken out and London's East End children are being evacuated to the country — among them William Beech. Willie, a skinny, filthy nine-year-old is frightened of everything and everyone. He is dumped on crusty old Tom Oakley simply because his mother has insisted that Willie be placed near a church, and Tom lives next to the graveyard. Willie is disturbed by the peace and quiet of the village of Little Weirwold and terrified of the animals he encounters, even Tom's friendly collie, Sammy, and plodding old Dobbs, Tom's horse.

Tom is equally disturbed. For forty years (ever since his wife and infant child died) he has kept aloof from the other people in the village, but now Willie's needs force him to turn to them for help. Willie has been badly beaten by his mother, so that means a visit to Dr Little and his wife, Nancy. Willie desperately needs new clothes, so that means talking to shopkeepers. And now, for Willie's sake, he must dig an air-raid shelter in his backyard. With help from the Fletcher family, they manage to get it almost finished, but then Tom goes off to the village hall to a meeting called by the Vicar, Mr Peters. He leaves Willie to finish off the roof of the Anderson shelter (as it's called). Willie is in the middle of smoothing over the muddy earth when he looks up to see a wiry, curly-haired boy whom he's noticed earlier in the Post Office.

The boy speaks . . .

"Hello!" he said brightly, grasping Willie's hand. There was a loud squelching of mud as he shook it.

"Sorry!" gasped Willie in embarrassment.

The strange boy grinned and wiped it on the seat of his shorts. "You're William Beech, aren't you?" Willie nodded. "Pleased to meet you. I'm Zacharias Wrench."

"Oh," said Willie.

"Yes, I know. It's a mouthful, isn't it. My parents have a cruel sense of humour. I'm called Zach for short."

The strange boy's eyes seemed to penetrate so deeply into Willie's that he felt sure he could read his thoughts. He averted his gaze, and began hurriedly to cover the Anderson again.

"I say, can I help? I'd like to."

Willie was quite taken aback at being asked.

"I'm rather good at it, actually," he continued proudly. "I've given a hand at the creation of several. I wouldn't mess it up."

"Yeh," replied Willie quietly, "if you want."

"Thanks. I say," he said as he dumped a handful of earth on the side of the shelter. "I'll show you around. Do you like exploring?"

Willie shrugged his shoulders. "I dunno."

"Is it your first visit to the country?" But before Willie could reply the boy was already chattering on. "It's not mine exactly. I've had odd holidays with friends and my parents but this is the first time I've actually sort of *lived* in the country. I've read books that are set in the country and, of course, poems, and I've lived in towns *near* the country and gone into the country on Sundays or when there was no school." He stopped and there was a moment of silence as they carried on working. "You've not been here long, have you?" he asked after a while. Willie shook his head. "Else I'm sure I would have seen you around. You're different."

Willie raised his head nervously. "Am I?"

"Yes, I sensed that as soon as I saw you. There's someone who's a bit of a loner, I thought, an independent sort of a soul like myself, perhaps." Willie glanced quickly at him. He felt quite tongue-tied. "You're living with Mr Oakley, aren't you?" He nodded. "He's a bit of a recluse, I believe."

"Wot?" said Willie.

"A recluse. You know, keeps himself to himself."

"Oh."

"I say," said Zach suddenly. "We'll be at school together, won't we?"

He shrugged his shoulders again. "I dunno." He felt somewhat bewildered. He couldn't understand this exuberant friendliness in a boy he'd only had a glimpse of twice. It was all too fast for him to take in.

"I expect you think I'm a bit forward," remarked Zach.

"Wot?"

"Forward. You know. But you see my parents work in the theatre and I'm so used to moving from town to town that I can't afford to waste time. As soon as I see someone I like, I talk to them."

Willie almost dropped the clod of earth he was holding. No one had ever said that they liked him. He'd always accepted that no one did. Even his Mum said she only liked him when he was quiet and still. For her to like him he had to make himself invisible. He hurriedly put the earth on to the shelter.

"I say," said Zach after a while. "I can't reach the top. Is there a ladder indoors?" Willie nodded. "Where is it?"

"In the hall. It's Mister Tom's."

"He won't mind, will he?"

"I dunno," whispered Willie, a little panic-stricken.

"I'll take the blame if there's any trouble," said Zach. "I say, maybe we can finish it and put the ladder back before he returns. It'll be a surprise then, won't it?" Willie nodded dumbly. "Lead the way, then," cried Zach. "On, on, on," and with that they made their way towards the back door.

Meanwhile, after walking in almost total darkness with no lights to guide him save the fast-darkening sky, Tom reached the village hall. It came as quite a shock to enter the brightly-lit building. He shaded his eyes and blinked for a few seconds until he had adjusted to the change. There were far more people than he had anticipated and the buzz of excited chatter was quite deafening. He tried to slip in unnoticed but it was too late. He had already been spotted by Mrs Miller.

"Well, Mr Oakley," she burbled. "This is a surprise!"

He turned to frown her into silence.

She was decked out in her Sunday best. A pink pillar-box hat was perched precariously on her head, and pinned to its side was a large artificial purple flower. It hung half-suspended over her mottled pudgy cheeks. The hat could have been a continuation of her face, Tom thought, the colours were so similar.

He cleared his throat. "Vicar called the meeting, so here I am."

"Yes, of course," said Mrs Miller.

He glanced quickly round the hall. Some of the older boys were already in uniform, their buff-coloured boxes slung over their shoulders. Mr Peters, Charlie Ruddles and Mr Bush were seated in the front with Mr Thatcher and Mr Butcher. He slipped quietly to the back of the hall, catching sight of Nancy and Dr Little and acknowledged their presence with a slight gesture of his hand.

He attempted to stand inconspicuously in a corner but it was useless, for most of the villagers nudged one another and turned to stare in his direction. Tom, as Zach said, kept himself to himself. He didn't hold with meetings or village functions. Since his wife Rachel's, death he hadn't joined in any of the social activities in Little Weirwold. In his grief he had cut himself off from people and when he had recovered he had lost the habit of socializing.

"Evenin', Mr Oakley," said Mrs Fletcher, who was busy knitting in the back row. "Left the boy, has you?"

"With Sam," he added, by way of defence.

He had been surprised at Sam's willingness to stay, and had even felt a flicker of jealousy when he had flopped contentedly down in the grass beside the boy's feet.

Although most wireless owners had opened their doors so that people could listen to the King's message, Mr Peters talked about it for those who had missed it. He mentioned the regulations regarding the blackout and the carrying of gas-masks, and Mr Thatcher, the tall ginger-haired father of the twin girls and their dark-haired sister, spoke about the procedure of action during an air raid.

Gumboots and oilskins were given out and ordered for volunteers.

It was decided that the First Aid Post would be at Doctor and Nancy Little's cottage and that the village hall was to be the Rest Centre.

Mrs Miller threw her puffy arm into the air and volunteered to run a canteen for any troops that might pass through. This suggestion was greeted with howls of laughter at the idea of anyone bothering to take a route that included Little Weirwold. However, Lilian Peters, seeing how hurt Mrs Miller was, said that she thought that it was a good idea and after suggesting that a weekly gathering of the evacuated mothers and their infants would also be an excellent idea, Mrs Miller sat down beaming, because she believed she had thought of it herself.

Mr Bush announced that Mrs Black had agreed to help at the school as there would be an extra seventy children attending. She was a quietly-spoken old lady who had been retired for seven years.

"Goin' to have her hands full with some of that town lot," Tom remarked to himself.

Several people volunteered for being special constables but Tom remained silent. His life had been well-ordered and reasonably happy, he thought, by minding his own business. The last thing he wanted was to turn himself into a do-gooder, but he realized very quickly that most of the volunteers were genuinely and sincerely opening their hearts and homes.

Mr Thatcher stood up to talk about fire-watching duties.

"No one is allowed to do more than forty-eight hours a month," he said. "Just a couple of hours a day."

Tom raised his arm.

Mr Peters looked towards the back of the hall in surprise. "Yes, Tom?" he asked. "Did you wish to say something?"

"I'm volunteering, like," he said.

"I beg yer pardon," said Mr Thatcher in amazement.

"I'll do the two hours a day. Early in the mornin' like, or tea- time. Can't leave the boy alone at night."

"No, no, of course not," and his name was hurriedly put down.

There was a murmur of surprise and enthusiasm in the hall. A tall, angular figure stood up. It was Emilia Thorne.

"Put mine there too," she said, "and while I'm about it, anyone who would like to join our Amateur Dramatics Group is very welcome. Meetings now on Thursdays, which means you can still attend practices at the First Aid Post on Wednesdays."

Soon a dozen or so hands were raised and after their names had been written down and details of what their duties would involve the meeting was brought to a close.

It was dark when Tom stepped out of the hall. He strod away towards the arched lane while the sound of chatter and laughter behind him gradually faded. He recollected, in his mild stupor, that Mrs Fletcher and Emilia Thorne had spoken to him and that the Doctor had asked after William and had said something about their boy being over at his place.

It was pitch black under the overhanging branches and it wasn't until he reached the gate of Dobbs' field that he was able, at last, to distinguish the shapes of the trees, and Dobbs and the wall by the churchyard. He swung open the gate and shut it firmly behind him. "Bet Rachel's 'avin' a good laugh," he muttered wryly to himself for not only had he volunteered for fire-watching duties, but he had also volunteered the services of Dobbs and the cart since there was news of petrol rationing. He strolled over to the nag and slapped her gently.

"I'll has to get you a gas-mask, and all, eh ole girl. Seems we're both up to our necks in it now."

The stars were scattered in fragments across the sky. Tom stared up at them. It didn't seem possible that there was a war. The night was so still and peaceful. He suddenly remembered Willie.

"Hope he's had the sense to go inside," he mumbled and he headed in the direction of home. He opened the little back gate and peered around in the dark for the shelter. He would have bumped into it if he hadn't heard voices.

"William! William! Where is you?"

"Ere, Mister Tom," said a voice by his side.

Tom squinted down at him. "Ent you got sense enuff to go indoors? Yous'll catch cold in that wet jersey."

A loud scrabbling came from inside the Anderson and Sam leapt out of the entrance and tugged excitedly at his trousers. Tom picked him up, secretly delighted that he hadn't been deserted in affection. Sam licked his face, panting and barking.

"It was my idea," said a cultured voice. "To keep at it."

"Who's that?" asked Tom sharply.

"Me, Mr Oakley," and he felt a hand touch his shirt-sleeve.

Tom screwed up his eyes to look at Zach. He could make out what looked like a girl in the darkness.

"I just thought it was a shame to go inside on such a night as this," he continued, "so I persuaded Will to partake of my company for a while."

"Who's Will?" asked Tom, bluntly.

"My name for William. He told me he was called Willie, but I thought that was a jolly awful thing to do to anyone. Willie just cries out for ridicule, don't you think? I mean," he went on, "it's almost as bad as Zacharias Wrench."

"What?" said Tom.

"Zacharias Wrench. That's me. Zach for short."

"Oh."

Willie stared at their silent silhouettes in the darkness, for what seemed an eternity. He could hear only the sound of Sam's tongue lathering Tom's face and a gentle breeze gliding through the trees.

"Best come in," said Tom at last.

They clattered into the hallway. Tom put the blacks up in the front room, crashed around in the darkness and lit the gas and oil lamps. After he had made a pot of tea they sat near the range and surveyed each other.

Willie's face, hair and clothes were covered in earth. His filthy hands showed up starkly against the white mug he was holding. Zach, Tom discovered, was a voluble, curly-haired boy a few months older than Willie, only taller and in bad need, so he thought, of a haircut. A red jersey was draped around his bare shoulders and a pair of frayed, rather colourful, men's braces held up some well-darned green shorts. Apart from his sandals, his legs were bare.

"You finished the shelter then?" said Tom.

Willie nodded and glanced in Zach's direction. "He helped."

"By the feel of it, you done a good job. How'd you reach the top?"

There was a pause.

"Wiv the ladder," said Willie huskily.

"Yes," interspersed Zach, "that was my idea."

"Oh, was it now?"

"Yes."

"You put it back then?"

"Oh yes. It might be a bit earth-stained, though."

Tom poked some tobacco in his pipe and relit it.

"Where you stayin then? You ent from round here."

"With Doctor and Mrs Little. I've been here for about a week now."

"Oh," said Tom. "I haven't seen you around."

"I haven't seen you around either," said Zach.

Willie choked on a mouthful of tea and Zach slapped his back. He flinched. His skin was still bruised and sore.

"I say," blurted out Zach with concern. "You're not one of those delicate mortals, are you?"

"No, he ent," said Tom sharply. "Least ways, not for long."

Zach glanced at the clock on the bookcase and stood up. "I say," he exclaimed, "it's nine o'clock. Thanks awfully for the tea, Mr Oakley. May I come round tomorrow and see Will?"

"Up to William, ask him."

Willie was so exhausted from the day's labours that he didn't know whether he had dreamt the last remark or not.

"Can I?" said Zach earnestly. "I've a marvellous idea for a game."

"Yeh."

"Wizard! Caloo Callay!"

With a great effort he attempted to pull his jersey on over his head. He tugged and pulled at it until it eventually moved over his nose and ears, causing his hair to spring up in all directions like soft wire.

"Phew!" he gasped, "I did it. Mother says I mustn't grow any more till she's collected enough wool to knit me a bigger one." He tugged the sleeves of the jersey down but they slid stubbornly back to between his wrists and elbows.

"Goodnight, Sam," he said, giving him a pat.

"William," said Tom, "see yer friend out."

Willie stood sleepily to his feet and followed Zach into the hall, closing the door behind them.

"Ow!" cried Zach as his knee hit the step ladder. Willie opened the front door. The sky was still starry and a cool breeze shook the grass between the gravestones. He shivered.

"Your jersey's awfully damp," said Zach feeling it. "Don't go catching pneumonia." He glanced cautiously round the graveyard. "Just looking for spies," he explained. "Look, about my idea. You know Captain McBlaid?"

"D'you mean Charlie Ruddles?"

"No," said Zach excitedly, "Captain McBlaid of the Air Police."

"Is he the prime minister or somethin'?"

"No!" He took another look around. "I'll tell you more about it tomorrow. Roger, Wilco and out."

Willie watched him walk down the path and towards the church. He pulled himself up over the wall and disappeared. Who was Roger Wilco and what did he mean by out, he thought. He stepped back into the hall and felt his way back to the living room.

In front of the range stood the large copper tub. Tom was pouring hot water into it while Sam was hiding under the table and eyeing it suspiciously.

"Don't worry, Sam. It ent fer you."

He looked down at Willie. "You'll be stiff tomorrer. Best have a good soak."

Willie stared in horror at the bubbling water and backed towards the table. He watched Tom lift two more saucepans from the range and empty them together with a handful of salt into the tub.

"Come on then," he said.

"Is it fer me clothes, Mister Tom?"

"It's fer you."

Willie swallowed. "Please, mister. I can't swim. I'll drown."

"Ent you never . . ." but he stopped himself. It was a stupid question. "You don't put yer head under. You sit in it, washes yerself and has a little lean back."

It took some time before Willie allowed himself to relax in the water. Tom handed him a large square bar of soap and showed him how to use it. He then proceeded to wash Willie's hair several times with such vigour that Willie thought his head would fall off. A drop of soap trickled into his eyes and he rubbed it only to find that he had created more pain.

After this ordeal Tom left him to have a soak and slowly Willie began to unwind. He held onto the sides of the tub and let his legs float gently to the surface. The gas lamp flickered and spluttered above him, sending moving shadows across the walls.

He gave a start for he had been so relaxed that he had nearly fallen asleep. Tom handed him a towel and after he had dried himself and had his hair rubbed and combed and had put his pyjamas on, he sat down on the pouffe by the armchair while Tom sat ready to tell him a story. Sam spread himself out on the rug between them.

"I'm goin' to look at the story first and then tells it in me own way, like what I done with Noah. That suit you?"

Willie nodded and hugged his knees.

"This is the story of how God created the world," and he began to talk about the light and the darkness, the coming of the sky and the sea, the fish and the animals and of Adam and Eve.

After this he made them both some cocoa and began the first of the *Just So* stories.

"I haven't read these for years," he said, leaning over to Willie. "Come and look at these pictures."

Willie rested against the arm of the armchair and listened to "How the Whale got his Throat". This was a slow process, for Tom had to keep stopping to explain what the words meant, and several times had to look them up in a dictionary.

Willie lay in bed that night, tired and aching, but the aches were very pleasant ones.

by Michelle Magorian
illustrated by Pat Sirninger

THE WAR OF THE BIRDS

 Brave were the Wibalu women, brave and strong. Clever too, for they had the only boomerangs in the whole world.

The men of neighbouring tribes were envious and they wanted the boomerangs more than anything else in the whole world. So why didn't they just go and take them? Because the Wibalu were not only brave and strong and clever. They had magic too. The death chants they made to protect themselves were so powerful no man could get close to them.

Finally one tribe decided it was time for trickery, for magic even stronger than that of the women. There were two men who could change themselves into other shapes. "White swans," said one, "that's what we'll be". "Yes," said the other, "and we'll fly to a waterhole near the women's camp. When they rush to see such strange birds, the rest of you can creep in and steal the boomerangs."

It worked.

The women ran to the waterhole, as planned. The men, who'd been hiding close by, seized the boomerangs and fled. And the women? Ah, they screamed with anger at their loss and rushed back to beat the white swans to death, but too late. The waterhole was empty.

Flying is hard when you're not used to it, and the men, still disguised as white swans, dropped down to a quiet lily-covered lagoon to rest.

Suddenly harsh cries of rage cut the air and out of the sky dropped several eagles. The lagoon was their home and they shared it with no one. They snatched up the swans in their powerful claws and flew with them far out into the desert. Then they raked the defenceless pair with those cruel talons and tore feathers from the limp bodies with their vicious beaks. And when the swans lay naked and bleeding on the hot dry sand, the eagles screeched their satisfaction to the world, then whirled away . . . and all was silence.

But from the north came a flock of crows. Filled with compassion, for the eagles had tortured and killed many an unwary crow, they plucked the feathers from their own bodies and let them fall in a soft, black healing blanket upon the miserable swans.

In memory of this, the true Australian swan goes dressed in the black feathers of the crow, with only the white feathers on the tip of its wings to remind us that once it was white. And its beak is red — the colour of blood.

An Aboriginal story, re-told and illustrated by Pat Edwards.

The P.O.W.

Twelve year old Patty Bergen isn't used to being liked. As a Jewish girl in a small non-Jewish town, Jenkinsville, in Arkansas, U.S.A., during World War II, she has a hard time fitting in. For some reason she cannot fathom, Patty's parents seem to dislike her. They notice her only to say what she's doing wrong and often punish her brutally. Their housekeeper, Ruth, is much more of a kind mother to her.

The family owns Bergen's Department Store and, while the other girls in Patty's class are off at summer camp, she helps out in the shop. Like everyone else in Jenkinsville, Patty is full of curiosity about the German prisoners of war who have been brought to work there. When they stepped off the train she was surprised how ordinary they looked — in their denim pants and shirts they might even be American.

One day the prisoners were brought to their shop to buy hats, and Patty sold some stationery and a brooch to one of them — Anton Reiker. She immediately liked him and felt he liked her. She awaited the day when they could meet again.

Ruth has just cut off the worst of Patty's new hairdo — an awful frizz of ringlets, put there by Mrs Reeves, the town hairdresser.

Patty retreats to the disused rooms above their garage — her secret hide-out, a place to escape, a place even her little sister, Sharon, doesn't know of . . .

I watched the late afternoon sun play with rectangles of light against the blue walls of the hide-out. The two rooms and bath had undergone a real clean-up, fix-up. And with the single exception of Ruth's dyeing that worn chenille bedspread a cherry red, I had done it all myself. Not even Ruth could have made the wood floor of the living-room or the linoleum in the kitchen and bath any cleaner or shinier.

A couple of times I was close to asking her to come see how I had fixed it up, but I never did. Partly it had to do with the problem of the missing steps. The other part was that I liked to think Ruth didn't know about the secret place. If she did, it wouldn't be so much of a secret anymore.

At the hide-out's back window, the one overlooking our Victory Garden and the railroad tracks beyond, a desk made from two sawhorses and an abandoned board held all my best books. I sat down, letting my hand prop up my head, and feeling the hair that Ruth had taken scissors against when I had come home from Mrs Reeves. At least the worst of it had been cut away. "Messing up something beautiful," she had said when first seeing me in my frizzled state.

Soon my mother and father would be home and Ruth would be on the back porch calling me in for supper.

Then from outside the window some movement caught my eye. A man with dark hair, denim shirt and pants, running below the railroad embankment. Soon the five-twenty to Memphis would be coming down those tracks, stopping at the Jenkinsville station only if there was a passenger wanting to get on or off.

But this man, and even from this distance there was something familiar about him, was running away from the depot. Maybe some poor fellow hoping to jump aboard at that point where the train slows before rounding the curve.

Then it struck me who he looked like. But it couldn't be — he's at the camp. It had to be him! Just like I prayed. God went and sent Anton to me.

The train blew a long whistle. In a single leap I took the steps. I won't lose you, Anton. Not now. I ran through the field faster than I was capable of running.

I could see the black-stencilled *P* on the back of his shirt. I called out, "Anton!" But my voice was cancelled by the great engine. Cupping my hands around my mouth, I tried again. "Hey! Anton!"

Still he didn't hear. But just before the train approached, he stopped and hid against the grassy enbankment. I ran my laboured run, waving my arms like an overburdened windmill.

"Anton!" His head swung around. He looked at me and then up the embankment, and for part of an instant I knew he was about to bolt across those tracks to his death.

"Anton, it's me — it's Patty!"

His face registered shock and then pleasure. An open palm reached out, waiting for me while overhead the train sounded like a thousand snare drums beating in four-quarter time. Our hands touched; I didn't let go till the train passed.

Directly in front of my father Ruth set down the platter of freshly fried chicken along with a skier's mountain of mashed potatoes. On the second trip from the kitchen she carried a basket of hot biscuits and a bowl of mustard greens. I wished that Anton could join the feast, invisible to everyone but me.

My father was saying, "I told him I might not be your biggest account, but I'm not your smallest. Not by a long shot, and when I order six dozen I want seventy-two pairs."

"You should have kept the six dozen you ordered," said my mother. "We're running low on men's dress shoes."

"Don't you tell me what I should 've done — not when I can get all the shoes I want at B.J. Walker's."

My mother blotted her lips with a paper napkin. "Oh, sure, you can cut off your nose to spite your face if you want to, but B.J. Walker or any other jobber is going to charge you another fifteen per cent. Then where will your profit be?"

He jumped to his feet, sending the chair to the floor with a crash. "Don't you dare contradict me! Think you're gonna treat me the way your God damn mother treats her husband?"

"Now, Harry, I don't know why you're getting so excited." Her face was a study in martyred innocence.

The insides of my stomach began swirling around. Did I overeat? I looked at my plate. With the exception of a hole that I had excavated in the potatoes, nothing had been touched.

'You know, God damn it. You know! And I hope to hell you croak on it!" His lips were pressed into a thin blue line and his hands were trembling with a rage beyond his ability to control.

"I don't know!" screamed my mother. "And I don't know why you're so mean and miserable."

My head began its circular rotation, matching in r.p.m. that of my stomach. Suddenly it came to me — I had a race to win. I reached the toilet bowl in time to see the mashed potatoes turned green gushing from my mouth, splashing down to the water below.

Since seven-thirty I had been listening to the sleep sounds of Sharon. Sometimes I think she's the wisest of us all. She isn't tactless like our mother or nervous like our father and she certainly doesn't always go rushing into trouble like me. I thought about all the trouble I could get into over Anton. My father would beat me, and if other people found out they'd never speak to me again unless it was to call me bad names.

Why did I have to see Anton running to catch that train? Twelve hundred people in this town and it had to be me. Why can't I be more like my sister? Sweet and nice and neat and with enough good sense to stay out of trouble.

Once, I figured out that the only thing that Sharon didn't have was enough words. But I could teach her. All kinds. Thin ones like *ego* and *ode*. Fat ones like *harmonic* and *palatable*. And I'd teach her some beautiful ones like *rendezvous* and *dementia praecox*. Maybe (just for variety) throw in some ugly ones like *grief* and *degrade*. And when Sharon knew enough words she could teach me all those things she was born knowing.

At exactly nine-thirty the yellow ribbon of light from underneath my parents' door went off. And less than ten minutes later the hard, grating snores of my father carried from the bedroom across the hall.

I put on my house shoes and robe before tiptoeing to the kitchen. He must be starving. In the fridge I found a bowl of leftover chicken that would make the beginnings of a great feast for Anton and me. How about mashed potatoes served cold? I placed everything into one of those brown grocery sacks Ruth was always saving, threw in some biscuits, tomatoes, and apples and turned the door latch.

"Who's in the kitchen?" my father called out.

"It's nobody, just me."

"Get something and get back to bed."

I unpacked the bag in the darkness and found my way back to my room. Then from a distance a train whistle sounded.

I waited till I heard my father's car accelerate out of the driveway before getting out of bed.

"Well, if it ain't the Sleeping Beauty!" said Ruth. "Morning to you, Miss Beauty."

I yawned a smile and then yawned again as I dropped into my chair at the table.

"How about a nice hot bowl of oatmeal?"

I nodded a Yes and then, thinking of Anton, asked, "Could I please have a couple of hard-boiled eggs too? And leave the shells on."

Spotting the *Memphis Commercial Appeal on* the table, I saw the biggest, blackest headline I'd seen since Pearl Harbor.

FBI SEIZES 8 NAZI SABOTEURS LANDED BY U-BOATS ON FLA. & N.Y. COASTS TO BLOW UP WAR PLANTS

Explosives Hidden by Nazis on Fla. Beach
Plan Against Alcoa Plant in Tenn.
Carried $150,000 Bribe Money

Two groups of saboteurs, highly trained by direction of the German High Command at a special school for sabotage near Berlin, were seized by the FBI. The men, all English-speaking, were carrying cases of powerful explosives and $150,000 bribe money.

Under cover of night one submarine released its saboteurs at Amagansett, Long Island.

In possession of the men was a list of special industrial plants they were to sabotage. Sabotage of department stores during their rush hours was also planned, to create panic and to break the morale of the American citizens.

The eight captured saboteurs are thought to be part of a larger underground network already operating within this country. The FBI has rounded up 27 men and 2 women from the New York–New Jersey area. Director J. Edgar Hoover says that many more arrests are imminent.

In Washington, Attorney General Francis Biddle said, "The Nazi invaders will be dealt with swiftly and thoroughly. The Justice Department will try the men for treason."

Articles of War proclaim, "Any person acting as a spy in war-time shall suffer death."

I felt my heart striking against the inner wall of my chest. I'm no spy! I'm not giving information to the Germans. But then again I suppose the Justice Department wouldn't stand up and applaud me for hiding a Nazi? He's not a Nazi! A technicality. A captured German soldier is close enough.

I turned to the inside pages in search of "Li'l Abner" while consoling myself that after darkness came Anton had probably hitched a ride on a freight train.

Opposite the comics there was a smiling soldier from Wynne City with a row of coloured ribbons on his chest. He wore his hat at a slight angle to show the world he wasn't afraid.

> S/Sgt. Clarence C. 'Red' Robbins, son of Mrs Mary G. Robbins, of 18 School St in Wynne City, Arkansas, died on 26 June from injuries received at Corregidor.

"It wasn't Anton's fault!"

Ruth brought in a bowl of oatmeal and a glass of milk. "It wasn't whose fault?"

"Nothing. Just something I read in the funnies."

She went back into the kitchen wearing a look of disbelief, and I went back to Red Robbins.

> S/Sgt Robbins was a member of the 1941 graduating class of Wynne City High School where he was voted 'Mr Personality'.
> He earned his letter playing football.
> His commanding officer, Capt Simpson B. Graves, wrote in a letter to Mrs Robbins: "Your son was a brave soldier and a splendid patriot."

A brave soldier and a splendid patriot. They were stirring words all right. When you help your country you're a patriot. But if you help the enemy then you're a — Fear pierced the calm of my stomach.

Ruth stood over me, hands on hips. "What you gonna do, girl? Eat it or meditate on it?"

I looked into her face deep below the surface of her eyes where the wisdom is stored. There are answers there all right. Good sturdy answers fashioned by Ruth to fit Ruth. Nothing there in my size.

"I don't know, Ruth," I said. "I just don't know."

By eight-thirty the vacuum cleaner was roaring in the living-room and the kitchen was all mine. I filled the paper bag with the best pieces of fried chicken, the mashed potatoes, two apples, hard-boiled eggs, and hot coffee tightly sealed in a Mason jar.

Outside the sun was beginning to warm itself for another sizzler of a day, and from the sandbox side of the house shrill sounds of Sharon and Sue Ellen made everything seem like always. I prayed to God that the hide-out would be empty too like always.

Inside the garage I strained my ears for sounds overhead. The creak of a chair? A footstep? But there was nothing. Then I remembered that the very last thing I had heard last night was the whistle of a train. He must have been on that train.

I stuck the sack between my teeth and started to climb up the stair braces. He has to be there. He wouldn't leave without so much as a good-bye. "Anton — it's me. Anton!"

Suddenly the door at the top of the landing swung open and a hand reached down to pull me up and in. "Don't shout my name!" Without touching the shade he bent to look out the window. "Don't you know better than that?"

"I'm sorry. I was afraid you'd gone."

"Well, I'm still here." Anton's frown began to melt into a smile showing a perfect set of white teeth. "And I am happy to see you." He smelled of soap and water, but his face showed the very beginning of a beard.

"I wanted to come back last night," I apologized. "But it wasn't safe. You knew I'd be back, didn't you?"

"Yes, I think so," he said, letting his eyes settle upon me. I turned my head away. I'm not much to look at.

As I ripped open the sack, spreading it flat against the desk like a tablecloth, I felt his eyes still watching me. "I'm sorry about not having a cloth, and I know I should've warmed the potatoes, but — "

"Please!" He lifted an open palm. "It looks good enough to eat." Anton pulled out the desk chair for me. Then, motioning towards the chicken, he asked, "White meat or dark?"

"Oh, no, it's all for you. I'm really not hungry." Grey eyes flecked with green looked up from the food. "Then we'll wait until you are."

I tried to calculate how long it had been since Anton had eaten. "I'll have something if you want me to."

Anton didn't let a hungry stomach interfere with his hunger for talk. Sometimes maybe a minute or more would pass before a bite of chicken was eaten. And when he spoke his face moved, matching the humour or intensity of his story. He talked about his parents' home three blocks from the University of Göttingen, a home of gables and gazebos where every Sunday afternoon at three, tea was served to professors, students, and long-time family friends.

Anton described his father, University of Göttingen history professor Erikson Kar Reiker, as being "a truly civilized man" for whom the war started back in the early thirties.

The president of the university had summoned him to his office. "Professor Reiker, these unfortunate statements, these jokes, that you are making about the new regime must cease! Did you actually tell your students that Chancellor Hitler sleeps with a Raggedy Ann doll?"

"No, Herr President, I did not. What I actually said was that I *suspect* Chancellor Hitler sleeps with a Raggedy Ann doll."

The president would not be put off. "Listen to me well, my friend. I will not jeopardize this university so that you may demonstrate your wit. If one, just one more of these treasonous remarks comes back to me, then you will give me no choice but to inform the authorities. These are dangerous times and one cannot make such statements and survive."

Anton took a swallow of coffee from the Mason jar. "Late that very night, something — I don't know what — woke me. I followed the light downstairs to my father's study, where I found him sitting, his head resting on his desk.

"He said that he was OK and nothing was wrong, but then he began speaking of his grandfather who had once been president of the university. Pointing to the books in mahogany cases that ran the breadth of the room, he said that some of these books were written because Grandfather believed that a president's job was to encourage scholarship. But our current president, he said, would be as comfortable burning libraries as building them."

For moments Anton just stared down at the bony remains of chicken. Then, abruptly, his forehead wrinkled along his hair line as he said, "It wasn't long after that, in the early summer of 1933, when students and S.S. men stormed through the university burning books."

"I wish people would have stood up to Hitler," I said.

"Some people did, but not many. My father chose acquiescence and life rather than resistance and death. Not a very admirable choice, but a very human one."

Anton went silent and I placed a red apple in his hand. "Tell me about your mother," I said. "Do you have sisters and brothers? And, if you don't mind telling me, how did you escape from the prison camp?"

He smiled. "You're a funny one, Patty Bergen. I'll answer your questions — then I'll ask one of my own. Yes?"

I nodded Yes.

Anton leaned back in the canvas lawn chair.

"My mother's minor virtues are limitless," he said as though he was warming up to the subject. "She sings on key, calls flowers by their generic names, and looks like she was born knowing how to pour tea from a silver service. And of her major virtues there are at least two — her warmth and her great sense of fun. She has the special ability to find adventure on a trip to the greengrocer. But primarily there is her warmth." He paused to brush away a smile. "I remember once, I must have been all of seven, running home from school, expecting her undivided attention. Instead the house was empty. There was a light on in the kitchen, pots of food simmering on back burners, and I knew she hadn't gone far or for long. And yet there I stood, brimming over with the most inconsolable disappointment."

Anton stopped for a moment, pressed his lips together before confiding. "It's funny, but I might feel something of that today. Now to your question — sisters or brothers? One sister, Hannah, three years younger whom I never had time for." He shook his head. "I'd like another chance."

"You will have one!" I said, totally convinced. "Just as soon as the war is over you can go back to Göttingen, start again. Will you return to medical school?"

"How did you know that?"

"You told me, remember? The first time we met."

"I'm going to remember that you store information the way squirrels store nuts. Yes?"

"Only if I'm interested," I said. "Well, are you going back?"

"I'm only concerned with now. And from now on I must be free." Anton breathed deeply as though the air outside barbed wire was different somehow.

"But can't you get hurt escaping?" I asked. "And wouldn't you have been free sooner or later anyway? Wars don't last forever."

A crease, like an exclamation mark, sliced Anton's forehead. "What do you know about sooner or later? Is a moment only a moment when you're in pain? For twenty-seven months I've been mostly bored to death and occasionally scared to death." Anton flung his hand out as though giving an emphatic good-bye to all of that. "Well, enough!"

Scared. Anton was a coward! "Our American soldiers aren't scared, do you think?"

"I think it's not in the best masculine tradition to admit it."

"How — I mean, why do you?"

Anton winked. "Because it's just another emotion."

"Sometimes I cry," I said, feeling exceptionally brave admitting it.

"And so do I." Anton began laughing as though he was having a good time.

"I'm glad you're here," I said. "I want you to stay safe."

"I will. There's no reason why the Americans should bother with one missing prisoner. An ordinary foot soldier."

He adjusted his gold ring, the surface of which had some sort of a crest. "Also, I'm lucky. Twice I've been so close to exploding bombs that only a miracle could have saved me. And so I've had a couple of miracles."

He took a quick look out the hide-out's front and back windows. "But suppose I am recaptured. What will the Americans do? Deposit me in the nearest POW camp where I'll have to wait till the end of the war. But in the meantime this day, this month, this year belongs to me."

Anton began carefully polishing his apple. "What was the last question?"

"I was wondering how you managed to escape?"

"The actual mechanics of the escape are not important," he said. "The pertinent point is that I was able to create a — a kind of climate that permitted the escape. Specifically, my deception was believed because it was built on a foundation of truth. Hitler taught me that."

I heard him say it. "Hitler taught you?"

Anton smiled. "I learned it by analysing his techniques. Hitler's first layer is an undeniable truth, such as: The German worker is poor. The second layer is divided equally between flattery and truth: The German worker deserves to be prosperous. The third layer is total fabrication: The Jews and the Communists have stolen what is rightfully yours."

"Well, I can see how it helped him, but I don't see how it worked for you."

"Because I had a rock-bottom truth of my own," he said, striking his chest with his index finger. "My excellent English. I let it be known that I had had an English governess. And this gave me the advantage of being considered wealthy. But I didn't have a good workable plan that would capitalize on my believed riches until I saw that pin with the glass diamonds — the one you sold me."

"Yes! I couldn't for the life of me figure out why you wanted it. So gaudy and not at all like something you'd like."

"I loved it!" protested Anton. "Because those glass diamonds were going to make me a free man. One of the guards was a simple fellow with financial problems. One day I told him my father would pay five thousand dollars to the person who could get me out of prison. The guard looked too surprised to answer. But eight days later he followed me into the latrine and asked, 'What's the deal?' 'Five perfect diamonds, each diamond having been appraised in excess of one thousand dollars, will be given to the person who drives me out beyond those gates', I told him. So he did, and I paid him with a dollar's worth of glass jewellery."

"I'm glad you made it," I said, "but that guard — he could get into an awful lot of trouble."

"I don't feel guilty." His hand rubbed across the slight indentation in his chin. "His concern was for reward; mine was for survival. But on the other hand, I wouldn't wish to implicate him."

I nodded. "Now I'm ready to answer your question."

His teeth pressed together, giving new strength to the line of his jaw. "I'm certain you appreciate the seriousness of what you have done, aiding an escaped prisoner of war. I was wondering why you were taking these risks on my behalf. Because of your German ancestry? Perhaps your father is secretly sympathetic to the Nazi cause?"

"That's not true! My father's parents came from Russia and my mother's from Luxembourg."

Anton looked alarmed. "I'm sorry. It's just that Bergen is such a good German name."

"It's also a good Jewish name," I said, pleased by the clean symmetry of my response.

His mouth came open. "Jewish?" An index finger pointed towards me. "You're Jewish?"

I thought he knew. I guess I thought everybody knew. Does he think I tricked him? My wonderful Anton was going to change to mean. As I nodded Yes, my breathing came to a halt while my eyes clamped shut.

Suddenly, strong baritone laughter flooded the room. Both eyes popped open and I saw him standing there, shaking his head from side to side.

"It's truly extraordinary," he said. "Who would believe it? 'Jewish girl risks all for German soldier.' Tell me, Patty Bergen — " his voice became soft, but with a trace of hoarseness — "why are you doing this for me?"

It wasn't complicated. Why didn't he know? There was really only one word for it. A simple little word that in itself is reason enough.

"The reason I'm doing this for you," I started off, "is only that I wouldn't want anything bad to happen to you."

Anton turned his face from me and nodded as though he understood. Outside, a blue-grey cloud cruised like a pirate ship between sun and earth, sending the room from sunshine into shadows.

by Bette Greene
illustrated by John Fairbridge

WAR HAS BEEN DECLARED!

WAR DECLARED.

ULTIMATUM TO GERMANY ON BELGIUM.

REPLY UNSATISFACTORY.

The German answer to the British Ultimatum was received last night.

It was unsatisfactory, and at eleven o'clock war was declared on Germany.

The following official announcement was issued by the Foreign-office at 12.10 a.m. :—

"Owing to the summary rejection by the German Government of the request made by his Majesty's Government for the assurance that the neutrality of Belgium will be respected, his Majesty's Ambassador at Berlin has received his passport.

"His Majesty's Government has declared to the German Government that a state of war exists between Great Britain and Germany as from 11 p.m. on August 4th."

THE DAILY MIRROR, Wednesday, August 5, 1914.

GREAT BRITAIN DECLARES WAR ON GERMANY.

The Daily Mirror

LATEST CERTIFIED CIRCULATION MORE THAN 1,000,000 COPIES PER DAY

One Halfpenny

No. 3,364.   Registered at the G.P.O. as a Newspaper.

WEDNESDAY, AUGUST 5, 1914

DECLARATION OF WAR BY GREAT BRITAIN AFTER UNSATISFACTORY REPLY TO YESTERDAY'S ULTIMATUM.

Neptune's imps. They are torpedo-boats steaming in close order to enable them to send verbal messages one to another by means of a megaphone.

Field-Marshal Sir John French.

Rear-Admiral C. E. Madden.

Admiral Sir John Jellicoe.

Field-Marshal Earl Kitchener.

Remarkable picture of a submarine rising to the surface. Are we soon to know what these unknown quantities are capable of?

There are four men—two sailors and two soldiers—to whom the Empire will turn in her hour of need. The sailors are Admiral Sir John Jellicoe (known as "the future Nelson"), who has assumed supreme command of the Home Fleets with the acting rank of Admiral, and Rear-Admiral Charles E. Madden, who has been appointed to be his Chief of Staff. The soldiers are Lord Kitchener, whose achievements are known to everyone, and Sir John French, probably the finest cavalry leader in the world, who performed brilliant feats in South Africa, "the grave of reputations."—(Bassano, Symonds, Russell and Gale and Polden.)

TO THE NAVY.

KING GEORGE'S MESSAGE TO OFFICERS & MEN.

"THE OLD GLORIES."

"SURE SHIELD IN HOUR OF TRIAL."

The following message has been addressed by the King to Admiral Sir John Jellicoe:—

"At this grave moment in our national history I send to you, and through you to the officers and men of the fleets of which you have assumed command, the assurance of my confidence that under your direction they will revive and renew the old glories of the Royal Navy, and prove once again the sure shield of Britain and of her empire in the hour of trial.

"GEORGE R.I."

The above message has been communicated to the senior naval officers on all stations outside of home waters.

Evening Chronicle

No. 19,768. [Established 1885] INCORPORATING THE "EVENING WORLD"

NEWCASTLE, SUNDAY, SEPTEMBER 3, 1939. PRICE ONE PENNY

Special

400 P.11

FOR LATER NEWS...

SUNDAY SUN
ANY OTHER SUNDAY PAPER

BRITAIN NOW AT WAR

"HITLER WOULD NOT HAVE PEACE"

PREMIER'S CALL TO THE NATION

"PLAY YOUR PART WITH CALMNESS AND COURAGE"

ROYAL BROADCAST, 6 p.m.

A state of war exists between Britain and Germany as from 11 a.m. to-day. The French Ultimatum Expires at 5 p.m.

OFFICIAL WARNING TO EVERYONE

What To Do During Air Raids

A NOTICE broadcast to-day by the Lord Privy Seal's Office states:—

In the event of threatened air raids warnings will be given in urban areas by means of sirens or hooters which will be sounded in some places by short intermittent blasts, and in other places by a warbling note changing every few seconds.

The warning may also be given by short blasts on police whistles.

No hooter or siren may be sounded except on the instructions of the police.

When you hear any of these sounds—take shelter.

Do not leave your shelter until you hear the "raiders passed" signal, which will be given by continuously sounding the sirens or hooters for a period of two minutes on the same note.

If poison gas has been used you will be warned by means of hand rattles. If you hear hand rattles do not leave your shelter until the poison gas has been cleared away.

Hand bells will be used to tell you when there is no longer any danger of poison gas.

DAILY SKETCH MONDAY, SEPTEMBER 4, 1939.

AND NOW MAY GOD DEFEND THE RIGHT: See P.

THE FASTEST EVER

Sir Malcolm Campbell & Mr. John Cobb

both used

K·L·G
SPARKING PLUGS

DAILY SKETCH

No. 9,464   MONDAY, SEPTEMBER 4, 1939   ONE PENNY

LATES WAR NEWS

Britain (since 11 a.m. yesterday) and France (since 5 p.m.) at war with Germany

Lord Gort leads British Expeditionary Force

Churchill in War Cabinet as First Lord

Hitler goes to the Front

Poles invade East Prussia

Warsaw alleges Germans are dropping gas bombs

LATE MESSAGES ON BACK PAGE

The King's Message

"STAND calm, firm and united!" That was the keynote of the message broadcast by the King to the Empire last night.

"In this grave hour," said the King, "perhaps the most fateful in our history, I send to every household of my people, both at home and overseas, this message, spoken with the same depth of feeling for each one of you as if I were able to cross your threshold and speak to you myself.

"For the second time in the lives of most of us we are at war.

"Over and over again we have tried to find a peaceful way out of the differences between ourselves and those who are now our enemies.

"But it has been in vain. We have been forced into a conflict. For we are called, with our Allies, to meet the challenge of a principle which, if it were to prevail, would be fatal to any civilised order in the world.

"It is the principle which permits a state, in the selfish pursuit of power, to disregard its treaties and its solemn pledges; which sanctions the use of force, or threat of force, against the sovereignty and independence of other states.

Must Meet The Challenge

"Such a principle, stripped of all disguise, is surely the mere primitive doctrine that might is right; and if this principle were established throughout the world, the freedom of our own country and of the whole British Commonwealth of Nations would be in danger.

"But far more than this—the peoples of the world would be kept in the bondage of fear, and all hopes of settled peace and of the security of justice and liberty among nations would be ended. This is the ultimate issue which confronts us. For the sake of all that we ourselves hold dear, and of the world's order and peace, it is unthinkable that we should refuse to meet the challenge.

"It is to this high purpose that I now call my people at home and my peoples across the seas, who will make our cause their own. I ask them to stand calm, firm and united in this time of trial. The task will be hard. There may be dark days ahead, and war can no longer be confined to the battlefield. But we can only do the right as we see the right, and reverently commit our cause to God. If one and all we keep resolutely faithful to it, ready for whatever service or sacrifice it may demand, then, with God's help, we shall prevail.

"May He bless and keep us all."

A copy of the message, with a facsimile of the King's signature will be sent to every home in the land.

The King about to broadcast last night.

Meet Christobel

Name: **CHRISTOBEL MATTINGLEY**

Born at: **BRIGHTON, SOUTH AUSTRALIA**

on: **26 OCTOBER 1931**

Started school at: **HOPETOUN SCHOOL, BRIGHTON, SA.**

Favourite subjects: **NATURE STUDY, READING**

Liked best: **MAKING UP PLAYS, DIRECTING + ACTING IN THEM**

Hated most: **GOING (AT FIRST), SEWING, SARCASTIC TEACHERS, PROJECTS**

Favourite food when young: **MY BIRTHDAY DINNER BY REQUEST: BAKED CHOPS + VEGETABLES WITH NEW GREEN PEAS STRAIGHT FROM MY FATHER'S GARDEN, FOLLOWED BY APRICOT PIE + CREAM**

Favourite food now: **SMOKED SALMON, ROAST DUCK, PEARS**

Best loved story or books when young: **SWISS FAMILY ROBINSON, CHILDREN OF THE DARK PEOPLE, THE SECRET GARDEN**

Mattingley

Favourite types of books now: ___THOSE WRITTEN FROM THE INSIDE___

Three things I love: ___BIRDS, BUTTERFLIES, BEING IN THE BUSH OR AT THE BEACH___

Three things I hate: ___PEOPLE FIGHTING, NUCLEAR WEAPONS, DESTRUCTION OF THE NATURAL ENVIRONMENT___

Secret wish: ___I'VE ALREADY SHARED IT IN "THE ANGEL WITH A MOUTH ORGAN" AND "THE MIRACLE TREE" – PEACE IN OUR HEARTS, IN OUR HOMES + IN THE WORLD___

Favourite riddle or joke: ___I'M BAD AT REMEMBERING JOKES BUT I LOVE ANYONE WHO MAKES ME LAUGH___

Ethnic background — parents: ___AUSTRALIAN___

— grandparents: ___AUSTRALIAN___

Autograph: _Christobel Mattingley_

THE ANGEL WITH A MOUTH ORGAN

This dramatic story was originally published as a picture book for young children. It is presented here for older readers to share in its intensity.

We had put the baubles, the tinsel, the lights on the Christmas tree. The angel was always last of all.

Peter and Ingrid started to argue and grab at its box.

"It's my turn!"

"You did it last year."

"I'm taller, so I can reach better."

"It's not fair!"

I said, "Hand piles!"

Peter put down his right hand. Ingrid put hers on top, I covered Ingrid's.

Peter covered mine and said, "Sorry, Mum".

Ingrid covered Peter's and said, "You will tell us the angel story again, won't you?."

Inside the box the little glass angel with the golden wing shone like a star against the cotton wool.

It started the year I wanted a baby doll. I'd hoped for a real baby, like our neighbour had. My mother wouldn't promise. So I asked for a doll instead.

But long before St Nicholas could bring one, out of the clouds the planes came, with noise like thunder and flashes like lightning.

They flew across our village. It became a garden of flame. The houses and the haystacks were like poppies, bursting out of their buds into glowing gold and orange. The church spire and the chimneys were like spikes of scarlet salvia.

When all the petals of flame had fallen at last, the village was like a skeleton. Buildings were black, animals were dead, people had disappeared. The earth was bare and burnt. But in the hearts of the people who were left the fire flowers had dropped their seeds — of fear and of hate, of courage and of love.

After the planes the soldiers came. They took away fathers, brothers, sons. But they didn't take our father. He laughed, "They don't want a one-armed bear in their circus!" And he hugged us with the arm he had left, almost as hard as he used to hug when he had both arms, before the planes came.

My father found a cart and Mother packed it with all we had saved from our burning house — quilts and feather pillows, three cheeses and some sausages, onions and a pumpkin, a bag of flour, some pots and plates and cups and knives and spoons, her best cloth which my grandma had made, and the cuckoo clock.

My father had his mouth-organ in his pocket. My sister had her books in her school-bag. I had my doll with the golden hair in my arms. And our neighbour, whose husband had been taken by the soldiers, had her baby snug in a quilt-and-pillow nest in the cart beside Grandma.

Father put our cow into the shafts, Mother tied on a bucket and a bundle of singed hay, and we set off. Walking.

I didn't know where we were going . . .

      how far we had to go . . .

      when we would get there . . .

We walked and walked and walked. And always the sound of the thunder and the glow and the smell of the fire flowers was behind us.

We walked until the cow lay down and died, and many other people who were hungrier than we were, roasted her meat and made soup from her bones.

We walked until the baby died, and Father scratched a hole under a birch tree and my sister and I gathered moss for its new bed and leaves for its blankets. My sister tore a page from her school-book and wrote the baby's name. She slipped it under the stone our neighbour put on top of the leaves and earth.

We walked until our neighbour and our last cheese disappeared one night. Mother and Father didn't say anything. But Grandma, who now had the whole cart to herself, said, "It won't do her any good". Two days later I thought I saw someone wearing our neighbour's boots and I was sure I saw someone else wearing her shawl. But Mother and Father wouldn't say anything.

We walked until the sun grew thin and pale, and we grew thin and pale too. The days shrank into long cold nights and our flour bag shrank too. The leaves turned yellow and brown, wrinkled and brittle, and so did Grandma. My sister and I slept each side of her at night to keep her warm. But often we could hear her teeth chattering as she called to Grandpa in her dreams.

One morning there was an empty space between my sister and me.

"She has gone to be with Grandpa," Mother said, as Father played Grandma's favourite tunes on his mouth-organ.

"Perhaps they're dancing now," my sister said. She took my hand and we danced the dances Grandma had taught us. Mother and Father danced too. Mother held Father's empty sleeve, because he needed his hand for his mouth-organ.

We walked until a wheel fell off our cart and before Father could mend it, some other people broke it up for firewood to roast an ox which had died. They didn't give us any. But Father said, "What would we be wanting with roast leather and burnt bones? And good riddance to the cart. We don't need it any longer. We'll get along faster without it".

He didn't say where we were getting along to. But we went on walking, each of us carrying a bundle which Mother had made out of the things left in the cart. I had the cups and the plates, and the spoons which rattled and the knives which poked me. My sister had the bucket with the pots in it. Mother had the food wrapped in Grandma's cloth. It wasn't a big bundle. Father had the quilts and the fat puffy pillows. He looked very funny. He sounded funny too, because the cuckoo in the clock would sometimes call from under the quilts, just as if it were at home beside the fireplace.

We walked and walked and sometimes the sound of thunder was very close. Then my father would play his mouth-organ. But even his merry tunes could not hide the smell of the fire flowers or drive away the smoke which made my sister cough and my eyes sting and run.

There were many people walking now and soldiers kept coming along in trucks, pushing us off the road. Then the roar of the planes was close and we could see them flying straight down the road towards us, with a spray of bullets blazing like lights on a Christmas tree.

My father pushed us into the ditch. Me and my doll. My sister on top. My mother on her. I felt the breath go out of me and my doll squeaked as Father threw himself across my mother. The cuckoo clock called, but I couldn't laugh because my mouth was full of doll's hair.

When my ears could properly hear again, the people sounds-were shouts and curses. And when I could lift my face out of the mud, I could see all the walking people standing up and stretching and wiping the brown off themselves too. But many of the soldiers were lying still. There was red on their uniforms and no one could wipe it away.

My mother said, "Thank God they spared us". But the soldiers in the trucks were very angry. They took away all the men and the boys from the walking people. They took my father.

We did not know why they were taking him . . .

where they were taking him . . .

when we would see him again . . .

We went on walking and we came to a place where we didn't have to walk any further, because there were big huts where the walking people like us could stay. There were many more children than in our village and my sister took out her books and started a school. I liked playing mothers and fathers better. The boys only wanted to play soldiers.

They all joined in, though, when my sister and I sang our father's songs. And they organized some good gangs to scout along the railway lines and around the station for coal which had fallen from the trains. They always took my sister, because she had her bucket and because she was always brave. But after I cried when the guards shot one of my friends, they always tried to leave me behind even though I had torn the sleeves out of my blouse to try to stop him bleeding.

I was good at finding acorns, though. My father hadn't nicknamed me "Squirrel" for nothing. And I never cried when picking hips off the briars, no matter how sharp the thorns were.

That camp was starting to feel almost like home, when suddenly one day we had to move. This time we didn't walk. We were put on trains. There were different people at the new camp and we didn't see some of our friends again. But we made new friends and we joined a gang which looked for turnips and potatoes out in the fields at night. The toes of my boots had worn through and I had chilblains, but I loved the patterns of the frost crystals sparkling on the clods in the moonlight.

We always sang our father's songs with our mother before we went to sleep, and I was glad she still had two arms and could hold us tight at once. And if I woke in the dark with the sound of other peoples' nightmares, I would hum the tunes to myself and think about my father.

We were moved seven times. Birthdays and Christmases went by, without presents or parties, candles or cake, and always we wondered about Father. I lost my teeth one by one, and others came, but not very

well. My sister grew tall, almost as tall as our mother. Our clothes were too small and our boots were worn out. We gathered leaves and grass and bark in the bucket to eat. And our mother's hair went grey.

The last time we were moved we went in cattle trucks. We didn't know where we were going. But the old thunder of planes and guns had been growing louder day by day and the smell of the fire flowers had been growing stronger.

The trucks were jammed with people and we children were glad when the train stopped at the edge of a wood and we were told to get off. We ran among the trees to play hide and seek and as I crouched against the trunk of a big fir tree, the planes came out of the clouds.

The bullets raked the train in long straight furrows, the way my father used to plough. And as I watched, the boiler on the engine began to spray in all directions, like a fountain in a park. It was one of the prettiest sights I had ever seen.

But the train couldn't go any more, so we clambered back into the trucks to fetch our belongings. The bullets had shredded my grandma's cloth as neat as coleslaw. And my doll had lost an arm.

We started to walk and I wondered where my father was and what he was doing. My sister started to sing his tunes. But I had a hard tight feeling in my chest and I couldn't sing. Then I heard a cuckoo call and I began to laugh. And I tied fir cones to my plaits and nodded my head and waved my arms and called, "Cuckoo! Cuckoo!"

I picked my mother a bunch of primroses and I didn't care if we couldn't eat them, because I was happy and I felt like flying.

We came to another camp which was even more crowded than the last, and in the huts there was no room for us or for the lady with the big tummy whom my mother had helped the last few days.

We had knocked on door after door, but the people all said, "Go away. There's no room for five more here. Go somewhere else".

We had tried almost every hut. It was growing dark and an icy little wind left over from winter was chasing us round every corner. Suddenly we saw a man open a shed door. He hurried in. My sister and I could tell he was important by his uniform. He jumped in to a car, looking very worried, and it drove away fast.

My sister and I ran into the shed. "It's empty," we called to our mother, quietly so that no one would hear. She came in with the lady and we closed the door softly. We smiled at each other in the half-dark.

We had the whole place to ourselves and there were only four of us. It was so quiet without the night noises of all the other people. Then the lady began making sounds we had heard before in the dark huts. My sister and I sang our father's songs out loud. Just before the light came again the baby was born and my mother wrapped it in the strips of linen that had been Grandma's cloth. I thought of the baby under the birch tree, and of my father, who could do almost as much with one hand as many people could do with two.

We all fell asleep then, but were woken quite soon when the sun was shining by the shouting outside.

"The war is over! The war is over!"

My mother jumped up and ran outside in her petticoat. My sister and I hugged each other and ran after her. The lady picked up her baby and followed us.

In the yard people were hugging and kissing, laughing and crying. Boys were whistling, girls were singing. Old women were crossing themselves and saying, "Gott sei dank!" over and over again.

All day long the sun shone and people laughed and cheered, sang and danced. In the evening they pulled down fences and gates and guard posts and made a huge bonfire, and my sister and I went with the boys up to the village church on the hill. We rang and rang and rang the bell. And nobody stopped us.

The next day everything was different. Everyone wanted to go home. Everyone wanted to find their husband, their father, their sons, their brothers. People began leaving the camp and new people started moving in, trying to make their way home, looking for mothers, aunts, sisters, cousins.

"When shall we go to look for Father?" my sister and I asked our mother.

"Not yet," Mother said. "It's easier for one than three to travel. We'll wait here."

So after being walking people and talking people, we became waiting people. We waited while the searching people came and went, day by day, week by week.

And everyone asked each other, "Did you ever see . . .?" and a thousand names and descriptions of big men, tall men, short women, stout women, naughty children, good children were exchanged and discussed. And people laughed or cried at the news they heard. The lady with the baby cried and went away.

Then a trickle of men started coming by, and the trickle grew to a stream. Gaunt men, grey men, lame men, men with one eye. And among them some women in the camp found the men they had described as big, strong, golden haired, laughing, and some children found fathers they did not know.

"When will our father come?" my sister and I asked our mother.

"When he comes," our mother said.

The green leaves turned to gold. Then the trees were empty and the snow began creeping down the mountainside. The stream of men dwindled and some of the waiting people's eyes grew empty too, and their hearts grew cold.

But we were the hoping people and every day my sister and I sang our father's songs, and they kept our hearts warm.

"Will our father be here by Christmas?" my sister and I asked our mother.

"Only the good God knows," our mother said, and her face was as thin and pale as birch bark.

The church bell was telling the valley that the Christ Child was coming.

"Let's go and see," I said to my sister.

We climbed the steep path through the Christmas tree forest and tiptoed into the little church. It was calm and sweet and coloured inside. The wind could not find its way in through the thick walls and the candles flamed bright and steady. The sun on the windows bathed us in red and violet and blue. And snug in the corner there was a crib.

Mary and Joseph, the shepherds and the kings were looking down at the baby.

I knelt down to see his face better, and I smiled, because he was smiling at me. "Look!" I said.

But my sister would not smile. She was angry. "It's not fair," she said.

I didn't know what wasn't fair. Was it that the baby was chubby and dimpled and happy, so different from the shrivelled, peevish little ones we had known? Was it that Mary had a beautiful blue dress, so different from our mother's darned black one? Or that Joseph had two arms? Or that the kings had gifts? Or that the cow looked so like ours which the hungry people had eaten?

Before I could ask, my sister had turned away. She grabbed the big brass candlestick and she hit the baby with it. Hard. Harder. Harder still. His little smiling face cracked and his chubby pink arms crumbled into plaster fragments.

My sister let out a big sob and ran from the church.

I ran after her. Calling her name. Begging her to wait for me. But she wouldn't. I tripped over a root and when I got up, she had disappeared.

I hurried back to the camp. I couldn't see her anywhere. But I didn't ask my mother. I took my doll and ran back up into the forest.

The sun had gone down behind the mountain and the trees were dark. I called my sister and sang our father's songs. But the wind gulped down my voice and made the trees moan.

Inside the church the light and colour had almost gone. The candles had almost died. I stole another from the box and lit it before the last one guttered out.

I took off my blouse and knelt down by the crib. Carefully I wrapped the plaster pieces in my blouse and when the space was as clean as I could make it, I laid my doll there.

Just off the path back to the camp I found a hollow under a big tree. I hid my bundle in it and covered it with pine needles.

Back at the camp our mother was hunting for us. "Where have you been?" she asked me. "And where is your sister?" And her voice was as shrill as the wind through the cracks in the walls of our hut.

My sister slipped in like a shadow and my mother did not even notice that my blouse was missing.

The snow came down in the night and in the morning all the valley was white and hushed. Then over the mountainside we could see the first of the searching people for the day arriving, coming down the slope like ants. And suddenly across the snow I could hear a mouth-organ.

"It's Father!" I called.

And I ran. And ran. Shouting. Falling in the snow drifts. Laughing. Crying.

I was the first to reach him. And he hugged me. And hugged me. And hugged me.

Then my sister came. And he hugged her.

And my mother. And they hugged each other.

And we all hugged each other.

Till Father said, "Careful. We don't want to break the other wing".
And he pulled something out of his pocket.

I thought it would be a bird — a blue tit or a goldfinch.

But it was a fragment of glass. And in the glass there was an angel.

Blue as the sky and gold as the sun.

My sister fingered the sharp edges. "Its wing is broken," she said sadly.

"But look!" I said. "It's playing a mouth-organ!"

"You could say so," Father laughed.

"Where did you find it?" Mother asked.

"In the ruins of a church," Father said. "And it's kept me company all the time I've been searching for you."

"And how did you find us?"

Father laughed again. "Whenever I went into a camp, I played my mouth-organ. And children used to come up to me and say, 'Those are the songs Lena and Anna used to sing. You must be their father. They said you had one arm and played the mouth-organ.' So I knew I'd find you somewhere, some day."

My sister said, "Can we go home now?" And our mother asked it with her eyes.

But our father shook his head. "There's no home to go to. And other people have taken our land."

My sister said, "It's not fair. After everything . . ."

But our father put his mouth-organ to her lips and her words turned into funny sounds. And we all laughed.

"We'll find another home," our father said. "You'll see."

And we did. Though it took a long while . . .

Ingrid put her hand on mine. "And you've put the angel on the Christmas tree ever since."

Peter put his hand on Ingrid's. "You unwrap it. You're more careful than I am."

Ingrid opened the box and picked up the blue and gold angel. It glowed like a star in her hand. "How sad its wing is broken. You put it on the tree, Peter. You're taller than I am."

Peter stretched up with the fragment of glass.

And the little angel with the mouth-organ proclaimed its message from on high once more.

by Christobel Mattingley
illustrated by Pat Sirninger

STRANGER IN THE VALLEY

This is an extract from fifteen year old Ann Burden's diary. Until a week ago, Ann believed she was the last person left on earth.

An atomic world war had destroyed everything she knew except the valley in which she lived. Somehow it escaped. There alone, trees and plants still grow, animals live. Ann's family — parents and brothers David and Joseph — had gone for help. They never returned. Afraid that crazed survivors might stumble into the valley, Ann hid out in an old cave close to the farm, but no-one ever came. Utterly, completely alone, Ann has spent the past year caring for the garden and farm animals, fetching supplies from the nearby deserted store and writing in her diary.

Then seven days ago a man appeared. He wears a radiation-proof suit and carries several guns. Not knowing how trustworthy or sane he is, Ann stays hidden in the cave and nearby woods, watching his movements through binoculars. She does not respond when he calls out, or even when he pitches his tent in her garden. Unexpectedly, Faro, her brother's dog whom Ann had thought lost forever, turns up and Ann sees Faro making friends with the stranger. Fortunately he does not follow when the man foolishly bathes in the nearby stream — a stream that Ann knows is radioactive.

Before night falls, Ann can see that the stranger is very ill . . .

May 27th

I am writing in the morning, having eaten my breakfast; I am sitting at the entrance to the cave with my binoculars, watching the house and the tent for a sign of life. So far there has been none, except that the dog went to the tent again, wagged his tail again, and sat down expectantly for a minute or two. He had an afterthought. He ran round the house, up the hill, and came to see me. Poor Faro. He was hungry, and now that he is home he expects to be fed. There

is plenty of dog food in the store, but of course I had not brought any up here, so I gave him a piece of cornbread and some tinned hash. I could be gladder to see him this time, since for the moment at least I was not worried about the man. I patted him quite a bit, and talked to him. After he had eaten he lay down beside me at the entrance and rested his head on my foot. That seemed quite touching because it is what he used to do with David, never with anyone else. Still, after only a few minutes he got up and ran back down the hill. He emerged at the house, where he sat down near the entrance to the tent. Although he likes me he seems to be adopting the man.

But the man himself has not moved.

I know he is sick, but I do not know how sick, and therefore I do not know what to do. It may be that he just doesn't feel very well, and decided to stay in bed.

Or he may be so sick he can't get up. He may even be dying.

Last night I would not have thought that would worry me so much, but this morning it does. It began with a dream I had just before I got up. It was one of those dreams that are more like daydreams; I have them when I am half awake and half asleep. I am somewhat aware that I am dreaming, and in a sense am making the dream up; but being half asleep it still seems true. I dreamed (or day-dreamed) that it was my father in the tent, sick, and then that my whole family were there again, in the house. I felt so joyful it took my breath away, and I woke up.

I lay there realizing that it was not true, but also realizing something else. I thought I had become used to being alone, and to the idea that I would always be alone, but I was wrong. Now that there was somebody else here, the thought of going back, the thought of the house and the valley being empty again — this time forever, I was sure of that — seemed so terrible I could not bear it.

So, even though the man was a stranger and I was afraid of him, I began worrying about his being sick, and the idea that he might die made me feel quite desperate.

I am writing this partly to get it clear in my head and to help me make up my mind. I think what I will do is wait and watch until late afternoon. Then if he still has not come out of the tent I will go down there while it is still light, very quietly, and see if I can see, without getting too close, how he is. I will take my gun with me.

May 28th

I am back in the house, in my own room.

The man is in the tent. He is asleep, most of the time at least, and so sick he cannot get up. He scarcely knows I am here.

Yesterday afternoon at four o'clock, as I had decided, I took my gun and went down the hill to the house. I came up behind it and walked, slowly and quietly, listening, round to the front. If I had heard any activity I was going to duck back and try to get away again without being seen. When I reached the front garden the dog came rushing up to meet me — I was afraid he was going to bark but he did not, he just sniffed my knee, wagged his tail and watched. I crept to the tent and looked in. It has a flap to close it, but that was hanging loose, partly open. Still it was dark inside. I could see only his legs at first. I crept closer, put my head inside, and my eyes adjusted to the dark. He lay on a sleeping-bag, partly covered, his eyes closed, his head in a mess where he had been sick. He was breathing, quite fast and shallow. Beside him lay a water bottle, a green plastic thing, knocked over and spilled; beside that lay a bottle of pills, large white ones, with the top off, also knocked over and partly spilled out.

The tent roof was only about four feet high. I knelt down and went in, just a little, so that I could reach his hand where it lay on top of the bag. The smell was terrible. I touched his hand: it was dry and hot with fever. Just as I touched it Faro, his nose in the entrance, whined, and at the combination of the noise and the touch he opened his eyes.

"Edward", he said. "Edward?"

He was not looking at me, or if he was, he was not seeing me; but I think he was looking at my gun, which I was still holding, because the next thing he said was:

"Bullets. It won't stop . . ." He did not finish the sentence, but sighed and closed his eyes again. He was dreaming; he was delirious, and his voice sounded thick, as if his throat and mouth were swollen.

"You're sick," I said. "You have a fever."

He moaned, and spoke without opening his eyes again.

"Water. Please give me water."

I could see what had happened: before he collapsed he had opened a bottle of water and some pills. In his confusion he had knocked them over. The bottle was empty and he was too weak to get more.

"All right," I said, "I'll get you some water. It will take a few minutes."

I got a pail from the kitchen, and ran to the stream where it flowed into the pond, where the water is clearest. When I got back I was hot and out of breath; I had filled it nearly full and it was heavy. I got a cup from the house and dipped it half full.

He was asleep again, so I touched his shoulder.

"Here," I said, "drink this".

He tried to rise but could not, not even on his elbow, and when he tried to take the cup he dropped it. I half filled it again from the pail; this time I held it, and lifted his head a little with my other hand. He gulped it down; he was really thirsty.

"More," he said.

"Not now," I said. "It will make you sick again." I did not know much about medicine, but I knew that much. He fell back and went to sleep again instantly.

The truth is, I did not know enough to take care of him. I had helped my mother sometimes taking care of David or Joseph when they got sick (grippe, chicken-pox, things like that), but never anyone this sick. Still, there was no one else, so I had to try.

I got a rag from the house and using some of the water I cleaned as well as I could around his head; I got him a fresh pillow and a clean blanket. I put the pills — those that were still clean — back in the bottle, capped it, and looked at the label: **Cysteamine**, whatever that is. The only medicine I had in the house (and the store) was aspirin and some cold tablets. But how could I know what medicine to give him anyway?

I thought that since drinking the water had not made him sick again perhaps he should eat something. But what? I decided on soup — chicken soup, since that is what my mother usually gave us when we were sick. I had left some tinned food in the house (it would have looked odd not to) when I moved to the cave, but there was no soup, so I had to walk to the store. I got some other stuff while I was there; I had already decided to move back to the house, but to leave the cave stocked for the time being, just in case. So I had quite a load to carry, and by the time I got back and got a fire going it was nearly dark.

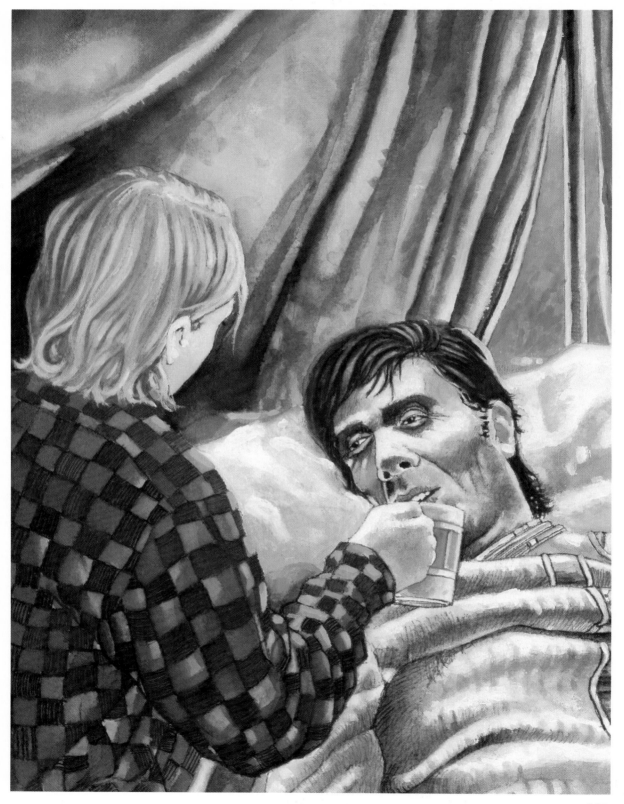

When I took the soup in to him I found, to my surprise, that he seemed somewhat improved. He was awake, and when I entered he stared, quite bewildered, and with some effort managed to raise himself on one elbow. Then he spoke to me consciously for the first time. His voice was still very weak.

"I don't know where I am," he said. "Who are you?"

"You're in the valley," I said. "You've been sick."

I put the soup down beside him. I had thought I would have to feed it to him.

"The valley," he said. "I remember now. All the green trees. But there was no one there." He lay back on the pillow again.

"I was here," I said. "I stayed in the woods." (I thought it better not to mention the cave.) "Then I saw you were sick, and I thought you needed help."

"Sick," he said. "Yes, very sick."

"I made you some soup," I said. "Try to eat it."

He did try, but his hand was so weak he spilled it from the spoon, so in the end I did feed it to him. He ate seven spoonfuls, and then said, "No more. Too sick." He fell asleep again. However, I think even that bit of soup did him some good; he seemed to sleep more naturally, and was not breathing so fast. I had brought a thermometer from the house to take his temperature, but I decided it could wait until morning. I touched his forehead. It was hot all right. From close up, in the dimness of the tent, he looked extremely frail.

I went back up to the cave, got my alarm clock, a lamp, this notebook and some other things, and came back to the house. I set the alarm for midnight; when it went off I reset it for two o'clock, then for four o'clock. Each time it rang I went out with a torch and looked into the tent to see how he was. Once he woke and asked again for water; I gave him a cupful. The rest of the time he slept steadily.

This morning I crumbled some of the remaining corn-bread in some milk and took it to him for breakfast. (I had to use powdered milk because the cows are still out. I will have to catch them now and bring them back in. Also the chickens.)

This time he seemed very much better. His eyes had lost the dazed look they had had earlier. He thanked me for the bread and milk and was able to spoon it out himself. After he finished eating it he actually sat up for a moment; then he lay back again and said:

"I need to find out what made me sick."

"I think it is because you swam in Burden Creek," I said.

"Burden Creek?"

"The stream across the road."

"You know about that?"

"I was watching — from a distance away."

"You know about the water."

"Nothing lives in it. I don't know why."

"I discovered that. But not until the day after I took a bath in it. So stupid to be careless, after all this time. I had not been in water for a year. I was too eager. Still, I should have tested. But that other water, in the pond, was all right. So I thought . . ." He stopped and lay quietly for a time.

Then he said:

"I might as well know. Could you —"

"Could I what?"

"Do you know what a Geiger counter is?"

"Those glass tubes you have."

"Yes. Can you read one?"

"No. That is, I never have."

I got the smaller of the tubes out of his wagon, and he showed me a gauge on one end of it, a small needle that wavered a bit when you moved it, like a compass. The dial was numbered from zero to two hundred. As he asked me, I took it across the road to Burden Creek. In the tent and crossing the road, the needle stayed at about five. But when I got near the water it began to go up. Standing back as far as I could, I held it a foot above the stream. The needle **shot** over — up to about one hundred and eighty, almost as high as it could go. And he had been **in** the water. No wonder he got sick. I did not stay there, but got back across the road.

When I told him what the needle showed he groaned and covered his eyes with his hand.

"A hundred and eighty," he said. "And I was in the water at least ten minutes. My God. I must have got three hundred r's. Maybe more."

"What does it mean?" I asked.

"It means I have radiation poisoning. Very bad."

"But you're getting better."

"It comes in stages."

He knew a great deal about radiation sickness; apparently he had studied it even before the war. The first part, being sick, lasts only a day or so, then goes away. Then the radiation caused what he called intracellular ionization, and that was the real damage. It means that some of the molecules in your cells are destroyed, so that the cells no longer work normally and cannot grow and divide.

It meant that in a short time — a day or two, maybe longer — he was going to get much sicker. He would get a very high fever, and since his blood cells were damaged and could not reproduce, he would also get anaemic. Worst of all he would have no resistance to germs and infection; he would be very susceptible to pneumonia or even the mildest impurities in his food and water.

"How bad will it get?" I asked. What I meant, but did not want to say, was, are you likely to die? He understood.

"Do you know what an 'r' means? It's a roentgen, a way of measuring radiation. If I absorbed three hundred r's in that stream I may live through it. If I got four or five hundred, well then it's hopeless."

He said all this in a very matter-of-fact way; he was calm about it. I think I would have been hysterical. However, I tried to stay calm, too, and be practical.

So I said, "While you are feeling better, you should tell me all you can about what I should do. Do you have medicine to take? What should you eat?"

He looked at the bottle of pills, still on the floor where I had put it. "Those won't help, not now. No, there's no medicine. In a hospital they give transfusions and intravenous nutrients."

I can't do that, of course, so what it amounts to is that there won't be much I can do, not until I see how the sickness develops. The only thing he seems sure of at this point is that he will have a very high fever and anaemia. It is likely, but not certain, that he will develop some kind of infection like pneumonia or dysentery. One thing I can do will be to try to prevent that. I can boil and sterilize everything he eats and eats from — just like a baby. When I get the cows and chickens back in I can give him fresh milk and eggs to eat; they are nourishing and easy to digest.

And if he is strong enough to walk a little tomorrow I will try to help him into the house. He can sleep in Joseph and David's room, on the bed. It will be drier and warmer in the house and easier for me to take care of him.

I've just realized that after all this I still do not even know his name.

by Robert O'Brien
illustrated by Edward Crosby

From Sticks and Stones...

A time-line of humanity's quest for the ultimate weapon.

BC

People use sticks, stones and burning branches as weapons against each other and wild animals.

1200

Homer records use of fire as weapon at siege of Troy.

327

Alexander the Great mentions use of flaming arrows.

AD 275

Roman general Scipio Africanus records use of gunpowder.

600

'Greek fire' (a form of liquid fire) invented by Callinicus, a Syrian.

668

Greek fire now used by Turkish army.

690

Record of Arabs using gunpowder.

1040

Chinese discover use of rockets as weapons.

1400

Use of cannon becomes common.

The era of the castle or fort as an invincible stronghold has come to an end.

1346

The Black Prince uses three small cannons at Battle of Crécy.

Caliph of Bagdad has unit of troops who fling burning naphtha pots at the enemy.

1300

THE GUNPOWDER AND CANNON AGE IS BORN.

1258

The French use cannon.

1247

Small cannon now being used in Spain.

1232

Chinese now using rockets as guided missiles.

1435

New guns called bombards invented. They shoot arrows, bolts or round stone balls.

Charles VIII of France sets up schools for gunners.

1453

Turkish Sultan, Mohammed II, uses 68 cannons at siege of Constantinople (Istanbul).

1500s

Korean admiral Yi Sunshin invents world's first iron-clad warship.

1520

Rifle invented by German August Kotter.

1525

First cannon made in England.

1537

Italian Nicolo Tataglia invents the gunner's quadrant to help in aiming cannon.

1540

Another Italian, Camillo Vetelli, invents the pistol.

1693

The Dutch invent the howitzer.

1620–30

Gustavus Adolphus of Sweden is first to combine infantry and cavalry.

1588

Spanish Armada defeated, largely due to fire power of British ships.

1584

Italian Federigo Gianibelli uses ship as floating mine to destroy bridge during war in Spain.

1580

Single-ignition shell introduced.

Naval gunnery makes its first great strides.

1759

Frederick the Great of Prussia introduces horse artillery.

1784

Henry Shrapnell invents round shell case full of lead balls.

1793

British introduce horse cavalry.

1775–1781

First contact mines used during American Revolution.

Note: The word *cannon* comes from the Latin meaning "hollow reed".

Ships of war now carry guns weighing up to 32 pounds.

1799–1815

Napoleonic Wars give various armies and navies plenty of practice.

1803

British Shrapn shells.

106

tO HYDROGEN BomB

1860

American John Ericson comes up with the idea of an iron-clad warship.

1849

Frenchman Claude Etienne Minie invents the long bullet which replaces the round metal ball.

1846

Italian, Ascanio Sobrero, invents nitroglycerine.

1831

American, Samuel Colt, invents revolver.

1822

Frenchman, Henri Joseph Paixhans, designs large-bore guns with explosive shells to use on ships of war and for coastal defence.

1812

US coastal defence also adopts explosive shells.

ts
sive

1861–5

Mines used against shipping during American Civil War.

1862

American Richard Gatling invents the machine gun.

1864

Smokeless gunpowder invented.

1866

Swedish chemist Alfred Nobel invents dynamite.

1866

Englishman Robert Whitehead invents torpedo.

1870–1913

Nations develop larger and more powerful guns. Rapid-fire guns appear.

1907

Frenchman Rene Loren begins research on jet-propelled robot bomb.

1920–39

Rocket experiments in many countries, but especially in Germany and United States.

1918

US Navy uses first flying bomb.

1917

American, John Browning, invents better machine gun.

1915

Germans use first flame thrower.

1915

First aircraft incendiaries dropped on London by Germans.

1914–15

WORLD WAR I Nations continue to improve existing weapons and develop new ones. Airplanes first used as war machines.

1936–39

Spanish Civil War. Techniques in aerial bombing develop quickly.

1939

President Roosevelt gives OK for experiments to begin on atomic bomb.

1939–45

World War II All weapons develop rapidly. Anti-aircraft rockets invented. Planes now carry bombs weighing up to 22 000 pounds. People now have weapons able to destroy whole city blocks. Germans use rockets to bomb London.

1942

Construction of atomic bomb begun in US.

THE NUCLEAR AGE IS BORN.

1954

US explodes hydrogen bomb. Development of target – seeking bombs.

1947

US Airforce develops bombs weighing up to 47 000 pounds.

THE ATOMIC AGE IS BORN

August 1945

US uses atomic bombs on Hiroshima and Nagasaki.

July 1945

First atomic bomb tested in US. People now have a weapon capable of destroying a whole city.

The word *bombard* comes from the Italian phrase for "thunder and lightning". The word *bomb* is simply an abbreviation of this.

CHRISTMAS DAY

25 December

Most joyous festival in the calendar of the Christian church, Christmas celebrates the birth of Jesus Christ in Bethlehem. Most of the world works from a calendar that numbers its years from that birth, history is divided into events that happened B.C. (Before Christ) or A.D. (after the death of Christ). Yet that date is probably wrong.

Historians have been investigating the period of Christ's life and death for quite some time and they've come up with the following facts, facts that they say prove that Christ was born on a different day in a different year.

First, there's the census mentioned in *The Gospel according to St Luke*. Luke states that this took place when Cyrenius was governor of Syria. The Romans were excellent record keepers, so it's easy to confirm that Syria (along with Spain, Gaul, Egypt and Palestine) was part of the Roman Empire at the time and that a senator with the rather pompous name of P. Sulpicius Quirinius was its military ruler. But they also state clearly that he ruled between 10 and 7 B.C.

Second, there's Matthew's account (written in his Gospel) which says that Jesus was born while Herod was king of Palestine. Other records tell us that Herod died, still king, in 4 B.C., so this places the date of Christ's birth some time before then.

Third, there's the evidence contained in ancient writings discovered by archaeologists. These give amazingly detailed information about astronomical observations that stretch back over thousands of years. In the year 7 B.C., it seems that the planets Jupiter and Saturn "met" within the constellation of Pisces. That means they moved so close that they had the appearance of a single, very bright star. Calculations prove that this would have been particularly visible in and around the Mediterranean and that the conjunction would have taken place three times in that year — 29 May, 3 October and 4 December. If we take the last date as the most likely one, the Magi (who were astronomers as well as wise men) would have had it clearly in front of them in the eastern sky as they rode out from Jerusalem to Bethlehem in search of the infant king.

The date of 25 December has always seemed wrong to those who live in the area. Local farmers move their flocks under cover before December frosts begin. It's highly unlikely they would still be out in the fields.

Put all these clues together and you get 4 December 7 B.C. as a much more probable date.

So who put us wrong? Historians blame the sixth century monk Dionysius Eiguus who first introduced the method of reckoning time by "the year of our Lord". It's believed he made a mistake in his maths and got muddled.

As for the day 25 December, well it seems the high-ups in the Church of Rome chose this day in the mid-fourth century because it coincided with an ancient Roman festival. Long before the Christian religion began, the Romans had honoured Saturn, their harvest god at what was called the *Saturnalia*, a rollicking carnival that lasted from 17 to 24 December. Since 275 A.D. also, they had celebrated the sun's birthday on 25 December. The Greeks also honoured the rebirth of the sun in a "Festival of Light" on the same day. So the Church officials decided to give Christians something to celebrate at the same time so they wouldn't be tempted to join in the pagan festivities. Up till now it had been usual to commemorate Christ's birthday on 6 January at the Feast of the Epiphany, so it was only a matter of moving it back a couple of weeks.

But none of this matters. What is important is that we know from all this that the events described in the New Testament were real. The story of the birth of the baby Jesus is a tender, heartwarming one, beloved of people all over the world. The baby grew up to become one of the greatest teachers ever known, one whom millions believe was truly the Son of God, one who founded one of the world's most powerful religions.

Yet the message Christ left behind was a very simple one. He preached the power of love to end conflict and hate. He demonstrated the strength of passive resistance, the way of non-violent demonstration. In a world where violence and wars often seem a way of life to millions, it's a message that's even more relevant today than it was in Roman times.

The Christmas festival brings with it hope that some day good will rule the universe.

Innocent's Song

Who's that knocking on the window,
Who's that standing at the door,
What are all those presents
Lying on the kitchen floor?

Who is the smiling stranger
With hair as white as gin,
What is he doing with the children
And who could have let him in?

Why has he rubies on his fingers,
A cold, cold crown on his head,
Why, when he caws his carol,
Does the salty snow run red?

Why does he ferry my fireside
As a spider on a thread,
His fingers made of fuses
And his tongue of gingerbread?

Why does the world before him
Melt in a million suns,
Why do his yellow, yearning eyes
Burn like saffron buns?

Watch where he comes walking
Out of the Christmas flame,
Dancing, double-talking:

Herod is his name.

CHARLES CAUSLEY